►

WORDPERFECT 5.1

THE POCKET REFERENCE

Mella Mincberg

►

►

►

Osborne McGraw-Hill

Berkeley New York St. Louis San Francisco
Auckland Bogotá Hamburg London Madrid
Mexico City Milan Montreal New Delhi
Panama City Paris São Paulo Singapore
Sydney Tokyo Toronto

Osborne **McGraw-Hill**
2600 Tenth Street
Berkeley, California 94710
U.S.A.

For information on translations and book distributors outside of the
U.S.A., please write to Osborne **McGraw-Hill** at the above address.

WordPerfect 5.1® : The Pocket Reference

34567890 DOC 99876543210

ISBN 0-07-881662-9

Acquisitions Editor: Cindy Hudson
Copy Editor: Kay Luthin
Word Processor: Bonnie Bozorg
Proofreader: Jeff Green
Composition: Bonnie Bozorg
Production Supervisor: Kevin Shafer

CONTENTS

INTRODUCTION

This pocket reference is a concise, comprehensive source for information on WordPerfect version 5.1. It is for the beginning or advanced user who is familiar with how WordPerfect operates but requires either a refresher on exactly what certain features accomplish or a keystroke-by-keystroke handbook.

There are two main sections to this reference guide. The first section gives some general reminders of how to sucessfully use WordPerfect and its powerful features. Topics include starting and ending a WordPerfect session, moving the cursor quickly in a document, editing your text, saving documents on disk for future use, printing the text on paper, and altering a document's format. Also included is a list of the function key and pull-down menu sequences that are used to access features.

The second section, which comprises the bulk of this reference guide, presents in alphabetical order a comprehensive list of WordPerfect's functions and features. It provides the sequence of keystrokes to activate each feature along with an explanation of that feature's purpose and applications.

The following conventions are used throughout this pocket reference:

- A plus sign between two keystrokes indicates that the keys must be pressed together. For instance, CTRL+END means that while holding down the CTRL key you press END and then release both keys.

- A comma between two keystrokes indicates that they must be pressed sequentially. For instance,

HOME, SPACEBAR means that you press HOME, release it, and then press SPACEBAR.

- WordPerfect features can be accessed either with function keys or pull-down menus. In this pocket reference the keystrokes are provided for the function keys; see "Activating Features" in the General Reminders section in order to translate these function key keystrokes into pull-down menu selections.

- WordPerfect function key names are listed in SMALL CAPITALS, followed in parentheses by the corresponding keystrokes, as in EXIT (F7), PRINT (SHIFT+F7), and FONT (CTRL+F8).

- WordPerfect menu items are listed by name, followed in parentheses by the corresponding keystroke—both a number and mnemonic character—that will invoke that item, such as Password (2 or P) or Define (6 or D). (Some menu items are invoked only by a number or mnemonic character, but not both.)

Quick answers are easy to find with this pocket reference. If you should require more in-depth information on the Word-Perfect program, refer to additional Osborne/McGraw-Hill sources, such as *WordPerfect 5.1 Made Easy,* also written by this author.

GENERAL REMINDERS

This section describes the procedures you should keep in mind to work effectively with WordPerfect and avoid potential problems.

► STARTING AND ENDING A WORDPERFECT SESSION

The master WordPerfect disks contain compressed files that cannot be accessed until the files are expanded during installation. You must therefore install WordPerfect on a hard disk or on floppy disks before you use the WordPerfect program. To run the Installation program, insert the Install/Learn/Utilities 1 disk into drive A and at the DOS prompt type **A:IN-STALL** and press ENTER. Follow the screen instructions.

To start up an installed version of WordPerfect on a *hard disk system,*

1. Turn on the computer and load DOS.

2. Once the DOS prompt (such as C> or C:/>) appears on the computer screen, use the Change Directory command to change the default to the directory where you wish to store files to and retrieve files from.

3. Type **WP** and press ENTER to start WordPerfect.

For instance, in step 2 if you wish to change the default to a previously created directory named \WP51\DATA, your personal directory, type **CD \WP51\DATA** and press ENTER.

WordPerfect will then be properly set to store files to and retrieve files from your personal directory for the entire working session. (If WordPerfect will not load, then repeat the preceding steps, except in step 2 use the Change Directory command to switch to the directory where the WordPerfect program files are housed. Once WordPerfect is loaded, refer to DEFAULT DRIVE/DIRECTORY, CHANGE in the Functions and Features section so that you can properly set Word-Perfect to store files to and retrieve files from your personal directory.)

To start up an installed version of WordPerfect on a *floppy disk system,*

1. Turn on the computer and load DOS.

2. Once the DOS A> prompt appears on the computer screen, place the WordPerfect 1 disk (which you created when you installed WordPerfect) in drive A and a disk that will store your documents—commonly referred to as a data disk—in drive B.

3. At the DOS A> prompt, type **B:** and press ENTER to change the default drive.

4. Type **A:WP** and press ENTER to start WordPerfect.

5. When prompted to do so, replace the WordPerfect 1 disk with the WordPerfect 2 disk.

Step 3, changing the default to drive B, properly sets Word-Perfect to store your data (document) files to and retrieve files from the data disk for the entire working session.

When starting up WordPerfect, you have the ability to activate special startup options that could make your working

session more productive. Refer to START-UP (SLASH) OP-
TIONS in the Functions and Features section for a complete
list of these options.

You may encounter the following message when loading
WordPerfect: "Are other copies of WordPerfect currently
running? (Y/N)." This message appears if, during your most
recent WordPerfect working session, you experienced a power or machine failure or turned off the computer without
exiting WordPerfect properly (described next). To load
WordPerfect normally, type **N** for No in response to the
message.

Always exit WordPerfect properly before you turn off
your computer. This allows the program to close its own
temporary files, which are created each time you start up
WordPerfect. To exit WordPerfect,

1. Press the EXIT (F7) key.

2. Either type **Y** to save the document on screen, in
which case you must indicate a filename, or type **N** to
exit without saving the document.

3. Type **Y** to exit WordPerfect.

Once you see the DOS prompt on screen (such as A>, B>,
C>, or C:\>), you are ready to turn off your computer or start
up another software program.

► MOVING THE CURSOR

Once you've typed a document on screen, WordPerfect offers
you a myriad of methods for moving the cursor within the
text. You can use either a mouse or the keyboard's cursor

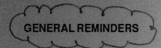

movement keypad. When using a mouse, move the mouse pointer on screen (▒) to the location where you wish to relocate the cursor and click the left mouse button. When you use the cursor movement keypad, the keys you employ depend on where you wish to move the cursor, as shown in the following tables.

Cursor Movement Left and Right

Key Sequence	Cursor Movement
←	One character left
→	One character right
CTRL+ ←	One word left
CTRL+ →	One word right
HOME, ←	Left edge of screen
HOME, →	Right edge of screen
HOME, HOME ←	Left edge of line (useful if the line is longer than the width of the screen)
HOME, HOME, → or END	Right edge of line (useful if the line is longer than the width of the screen)
HOME, HOME, HOME, ←	Left edge of line before any codes

Cursor Movement Up and Down

Key Sequence	Cursor Movement
↑	One line up
↓	One line down

Key Sequence	Cursor Movement
- (numeric keypad) or HOME, ↑	Top line on screen (or next screen up if cursor is on top line)
+ (numeric keypad) or HOME, ↓	Bottom line on screen (or next screen down if cursor is on bottom line)
PGUP	Top of previous page
PGDN	Top of next page
HOME, HOME, ↑	Beginning of document
HOME, HOME, ↓	End of document
HOME, HOME, HOME, ↑	Beginning of document before any codes

Cursor Movement with GOTO (CTRL+HOME) in Standard Text

Key Sequence	Cursor Movement
CTRL+HOME, *letter/symbol*	Next occurrence of that letter or symbol within the next 2000 characters
CTRL+HOME, ↑	Top of current page
CTRL+HOME, ↓	Bottom of current page
CTRL+HOME, #	Top of page #
CTRL+HOME, CTRL+HOME	Cursor position before last cursor movement command

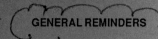
Cursor Movement with GOTO (CTRL+HOME) in Text Columns and Tables

Key Sequence	Cursor Movement
CTRL+HOME, ←	Previous column or cell
CTRL+HOME, →	Next column or cell
CTRL+HOME, HOME, ←	Leftmost column or cell
CTRL+HOME, HOME, →	Rightmost column or cell
CTRL+HOME, ↑	First line of current column or cell
CTRL+HOME, ↓	Last line of current column or cell
CTRL+HOME, HOME, ↑	First cell in column (tables only)
CTRL+HOME, HOME, ↓	Last cell in column (tables only)
CTRL+HOME, HOME, HOME, ↑	First cell in table (tables only)
CTRL+HOME, HOME, HOME ↓	Last cell in table (tables only)

► TEXT EDITING

When you are editing text, the methods you employ depend on the changes that are necessary. To insert text, simply position the cursor and begin typing; if you are in Insert mode, existing text will move to the right to accommodate new characters you type, whereas if you are in Typeover mode, existing text will be replaced by the new characters you type. (See INSERT MODE and TYPEOVER MODE in the Functions and Features section.) To delete text, the keys you employ depend on the amount of text you wish to erase, as described in the following table.

Deletion Options

Key Sequence	Text Deleted
BACKSPACE	Character or code left of cursor
DEL	Character or code at cursor
CTRL+BACKSPACE	Word at cursor
HOME, BACKSPACE	Characters left to word boundary
HOME, DEL	Characters right to word boundary
CTRL+END	Characters right to line end
CTRL+PGDN	Characters right and below to page end
Block text, DEL or BACKSPACE, Y	Characters/codes in highlighted block
MOVE (CTRL+F4) key	Sentence, paragraph, or page (see also DELETE TEXT in the Functions and Features section)
EXIT (F7) key	Entire document from the Typing screen (see also CLEAR DOCUMENT FROM SCREEN in the Functions and Features section)
CANCEL (F1) key	Previous deletion restored (see also UNDELETE in the Functions and Features section)

▶ ACTIVATING FEATURES

WordPerfect's many functions and features are accessed in one of two ways: with the keyboard's function keys or with the WordPerfect pull-down menus.

Use the function keys to access a feature by pressing a function key (labeled F1 through F10) either by itself or in combination with either the CTRL, ALT, or SHIFT key. The WordPerfect program is packaged with plastic templates that indicate function key names to help you know which function key controls which special feature(s). Be sure to place the template that is appropriate for your keyboard next to the function keys.

ALT=

Use the pull-down menus to access a feature by pressing ALT+= (or, if you have a mouse, by clicking the right mouse button) to display a menu bar listing nine items:

File Edit Search Layout Mark Tools Font Graphics Help

To "pull down" a menu from this menu bar, either use the arrow keys to highlight a menu item and press ENTER or type the mnemonic letter (denoted in boldface in the menu bar) associated with the menu. Or, if your computer is equipped with a mouse, you can select a menu item by moving the mouse to highlight a menu item and clicking the left mouse button.) The appropriate pull-down menu is then displayed down the screen.

After pressing a function key or selecting a pull-down menu item, read on-screen messages carefully for an indication of what to do next. WordPerfect may

- Prompt you for further information before activating a command. Enter the information that WordPerfect is requesting.

- Display a message in the form of a question, requiring a "Yes or No" answer. Type **Y** or **N** to respond, or, with a mouse, position the mouse pointer on the response you desire and click the left mouse button. (WordPerfect will always suggest a response, either Yes or No, indicated by the location of the cursor. If you agree with WordPerfect's suggestion, you can respond simply by pressing ENTER.)

- Present a menu that lists various choices. Select a menu item by typing the number or the mnemonic character that corresponds to that menu item. (The mnemonic character is usually denoted in boldface on screen.) Or, with a mouse, position the mouse pointer on the response you desire and click the left mouse button.

- Reveal a submenu of a pull-down menu. Choose a submenu item in the same way that you choose a pull-down menu item.

- Insert a code immediately, as is the case when you press the BOLD, CENTER, FLUSH RIGHT, →INDENT, →INDENT←, TAB ALIGN, or UNDERLINE key; a feature has now been activated.

Codes are hidden on the Typing screen; they are displayed only when you use the REVEAL CODES (ALT+F3) key to display the Reveal Codes screen and are shown in boldface and surrounded by square brackets. There are two types of codes: paired and open. Paired codes come in twos, with a Begin code in uppercase letters that marks the location where a feature is turned on and an End code in lowercase letters that marks the location where the feature is turned off, as in **[BOLD]** and **[bold]**. Paired codes are commonly those that alter a font attribute. Open codes are single codes that turn on a feature from the code location either to the end of the document or to the location where another code of the same type has been inserted. An example is **[Ln Spacing:2]**. Open codes are commonly codes that format lines or pages in the document.

To cancel a feature if a menu or prompt is displayed, press the CANCEL (F1) key (or press the middle mouse button); you may have to press CANCEL (F1) more than once to completely back out of a menu. To cancel a feature just after inserting a code, press the BACKSPACE key so that you can erase the code and thus turn off the feature. Should the hidden code prove illusive, display the Reveal Codes screen to view and erase the code you inadvertently inserted.

The following is an alphabetical list of function key names and a list of the pull-down menu structure—two independent methods for accessing the same WordPerfect features.

Function Keys

Function Key Name	Key Sequence
BLOCK	ALT+F4
BOLD	F6
CANCEL	F1
CENTER	SHIFT+F6
COLUMNS/TABLES	ALT+F7
DATE/OUTLINE	SHIFT+F5
END FIELD	F9
EXIT	F7
FLUSH RIGHT	ALT+F6
FONT	CTRL+F8
FOOTNOTE	CTRL+F7
FORMAT	SHIFT+F8
GRAPHICS	ALT+F9
HELP	F3
⇒INDENT	F4
⇒INDENT⇐	SHIFT+F4
LIST	F5
MACRO	ALT+F10
MACRO DEFINE	CTRL+F10
MARK TEXT	ALT+F5
MERGE CODES	SHIFT+F9
MERGE/SORT	CTRL+F9
MOVE	CTRL+F4

Function Key Name	**Key Sequence**
PRINT	SHIFT+F7
REPLACE	ALT+F2
RETRIEVE	SHIFT+F10
REVEAL CODES	ALT+F3
SAVE	F10
SCREEN	CTRL+F3
⇒SEARCH	F2
⇐SEARCH	SHIFT+F2
SETUP	SHIFT+F1
SHELL	CTRL+F1
SPELL	CTRL+F2
STYLE	ALT+F8
SWITCH	SHIFT+F3
TAB ALIGN	CTRL+F6
TEXT IN/OUT	CTRL+F5
THESAURUS	ALT+F1
UNDERLINE	F8

Pulldown Menus

File	Edit	Search
Retrieve	Move/Cut	Forward
Save	Copy	Backward
Text In	Paste	Next
Text Out	Append	Previous
Password	Delete	Reverse
List Files	Undelete	Extended
Summary	Block	Goto
Print	Select	
Setup	Comment	
Goto DOS	Convert Case	
Exit	Protect Block	
	Switch Document	
	Window	
	Reveal Codes	

Layout	Mark	Tools
Line	Index	Speller
Page	Table of	Thesaurus
Document	Contents	Macro
Other	List	Date Text
Columns	Cross Reference	Date Code
Tables	Table of	Date Format
Math	Authorities	Outline
Footnote	Define	Paragraph Number
Endnote	Generate	Define
Justify	Master Documents	Merge Codes
Align	Subdocument	Merge
Styles	Document Compare	Sort
		Line Draw

Font	**Graphics**	**Help**
Base Font	Figure	Help
Normal	Table Box	Index
Appearance	Text Box	Template
Superscript	User Box	
Subscript	Equation	
Fine	Line	
Small		
Large		
Very Large		
Extra Large		
Print Color		
Characters		

▶ INITIAL SETTINGS

The WordPerfect program was designed with certain default settings that control 1) how certain functions and features should operate, 2) how your WordPerfect Typing screen appears, and 3) how all documents should be formatted. You can permanently alter these default settings via the Setup menu; refer to SETUP in the Functions and Features section for further details.

To check a current setting for a particular function or feature, proceed as if you plan to change that setting. The current setting will be displayed on whatever menu is used to change that setting. You can then use the CANCEL (F1) key to back out of the menu without altering the current setting.

► CHANGING A DOCUMENT'S FORMAT

All WordPerfect documents are initially formatted based on default settings. Using the FORMAT key, you can change a variety of default format settings at any time and as many times as desired for a single document.

When you make format changes such as a modification in margin or tab settings, WordPerfect will prompt you for a measurement. You can indicate your measurement by typing a number followed by a character that indicates the number's unit of measure—" or **i** for inches, **c** for centimeters, **p** for points (there are 72 points to an inch), **w** for 1200ths of an inch, **h** for version 4.2 horizontal units (columns), or **v** for version 4.2 vertical units (lines). For instance, type **24p** to indicate 24 points. If you type in a number without also indicating its unit of measure, WordPerfect will assume you mean inches unless you alter the Units of Measure default; see UNITS OF MEASURE in the Functions and Features section.

Each time you change a specific format setting, you insert a code into the document. Therefore, it is essential to position the cursor properly before initiating a format change. You can position the cursor on a document's Initial Codes screen or at the top of the document itself to initiate a format change starting at the top of the document. You can also position the cursor somewhere within the document to initiate a format change starting at that location. To abort a format change, you must find and delete the hidden codes you inserted.

Certain of WordPerfect's formatting features (such as full justification) take effect at the printer but are not displayed on the Typing screen. Use the Reveal Codes feature to verify that the feature has been activated, or use the View Document feature to see on the screen just how the document will appear when printed (as described in VIEW DOCUMENT in the Functions and Features section).

BLOCKING TEXT

You can activate certain WordPerfect features on only a specific portion of text. To do so, first use the BLOCK (ALT+F4) key or use a mouse to highlight that text in reverse video. You are then ready to press the function key that will activate the feature for only the highlighted text. (See also BLOCK and MOUSE in the Functions and Features section.)

Be aware that, with several function keys, a different menu appears with the Block feature on (you pressed the BLOCK key first) than appear with Block off. For instance, you activate a different feature if you press BLOCK (ALT+F4) followed by SWITCH (SHIFT+F3) than if you press SWITCH (SHIFT+F3) by itself.

With pull-down menus, square brackets surrounding sub-menu items signify that the item cannot be selected at the present time because of the status of the Block feature. Certain items can be selected only with Block on, while others can be selected only with Block off.

22

► SAVING AND RETRIEVING FILES

Before retrieving a new file to the screen, always clear the screen of any previous document you were typing or editing. You clear the screen with the EXIT (F7) key. The only time you should not clear the screen before retrieving another file is when you wish to combine files together on screen.

As you're typing a document, save that file on disk frequently (every 15 minutes or so) to avoid losing hours of work to a power failure. (This can be accomplished by WordPerfect if you activate the Timed Backup option; see BACKUP in the Functions and Features section.) Be sure to save the file again when the document is complete and before you clear the screen or exit WordPerfect.

Documents are stored on disk in a file with a filename of your choosing. A filename can contain one to eight characters— letters, numbers, or symbols, including these:

! @ # $ % & ( ) - { } / ' '

The filename can also have an optional file extension, which is separated from the filename by a period (.) and can contain one to three characters. Examples of acceptable filenames are MEMO, MEMO1, MEMO1.HBJ, and MEMO#1.HBJ.

Once you have stored a document on disk, make a second copy of that file on a separate disk. That way, hard disk users will be protected if a hard disk is accidentally formatted or "crashes," meaning that all documents on the disk are erased. Similarly, floppy disk users will be protected if a floppy disk is misplaced, ruined, or loses documents due to a mechanical malfunction.

▶ PRINTING

There are two general categories of printing: from screen or from disk. Printing from screen means that WordPerfect prints out the version of a document displayed on the screen. Printing from disk means that WordPerfect prints the version of a document stored on disk, regardless of what is on screen.

If you print a document and the document's format is incorrect, the culprit could be a hidden code you inserted accidentally. Use the Reveal Codes feature to see how your document has been formatted and to uncover and correct the problem.

If you try to print a document but the printer doesn't begin, check the Printer Control menu. (See CONTROL PRINTER in the Functions and Features section.) Information under the headings "Status" and "Message" often indicate the problem, which may be a simple case of the printer not being turned on or the cable that connects the computer to the printer being cracked.

FUNCTIONS AND FEATURES: ALPHABETICAL LIST

The following is an alphabetical list of WordPerfect features and functions. Included for each entry is the key sequence that activates the feature, and an explanation of that feature's purpose and applications.

After activating a feature, use the ENTER or EXIT (F7) key to return to the document on screen.

▶ ADDITION

See MATH COLUMNS and TABLES

▶ ADVANCE

Vertical

FORMAT (SHIFT+F8) key
Other (4 or O)
Advance (1 or A)
Up (1 or U), Down (2 or D), or Line (3 or I)

Directs the printer to advance to a specific vertical position. This is useful for filling out preprinted forms, positioning text for desktop publishing applications, typing statistical equations, or printing two sections of text in the same vertical location.

For the Up or Down menu item, enter a specific measurement to move up or down from the current cursor position.

For Line, enter an exact vertical measurement from the top of the page. The text on screen is not affected, but the line indicator ("Ln") on the status line indicates the vertical location where the text will be printed.

Horizontal

FORMAT (SHIFT+F8) key
Other (4 or O)
Advance (1 or A)
Left (4 or L), Right (5 or R), or Position (6 or P)

Directs the printer to advance to a specific horizontal position. This is useful for filling out preprinted forms, positioning text for desktop publishing applications, typing statistical equations, or printing two sections of text in the same horizontal location.

For the Left or Right menu item, enter a specific measurement to move left or right from the current cursor position. For Position, enter an exact horizontal measurement from the left edge of the page. The text on screen is not affected, but the position indicator ("Pos") on the status line indicates the horizontal location where the text will be printed.

▶ ALIGNMENT CHARACTER

See DECIMAL/ALIGN CHARACTER

▶ ALPHABETIZE TEXT

See SORT AND SELECT

APPEARANCE

FONT (CTRL+F8) key
Appearance (2 or A)
Bold (1 or B), Underline (2 or U), Double Underline
    (3 or D), Italics (4 or I), Outline (5 or O),
    Shadow (6 or A), Small Caps (7 or C), Redline
    (8 or R), or Strikeout (9 or S)

For a particular base font, alters the attribute that controls the *style* of characters at the printer. Appearance attributes include Bold, Underline, Double Underline, Italics, Outline, Shadow, Small Caps, Redline, and Strikeout (see these separate entries for more details.) Be aware that many printers do not support all of these appearance attributes for a given font.

To activate an appearance attribute as you type, follow the key sequence just described and then select a menu item to turn on the desired appearance attribute. (You can repeat the key sequence and turn on as many appearance attributes as desired.) Next, type the text, and then turn off the appearance attribute by either 1) pressing the right arrow key, 2) repeating the same key sequence as when you turned on the attribute, or 3) pressing FONT and selecting Normal (3 or N) to turn off all attributes if more than one is active.

To activate an appearance attribute for existing text, use the Block feature to highlight the existing text before following the key sequence above.

On screen, the text controlled by a given appearance attribute displays in a different color or brightness to distinguish it from normal text (see the section COLORS/FONTS/ATTRIBUTES.)

► APPEND

Block, Tabular Column, or Rectangle

Block the text
MOVE (CTRL+F4) key
Block (1 or B), Tabular Column (2 or C), or
Rectangle (3 or R)
Append (4 or A)

Attaches the highlighted text to the end of a file currently on disk. When WordPerfect prompts "Append to:", type in the name of an existing file and press ENTER. If the filename you enter cannot be found, the file is created for you by Word-Perfect.

Sentence, Paragraph, or Page

Position cursor within the sentence, paragraph, or page
MOVE (CTRL+F4) key
Sentence (1 or S), Paragraph (2 or P), or Page (3 or A)
Append (4 or A)

Attaches the highlighted sentence, paragraph, or page to the end of a file currently on disk. When WordPerfect prompts "Append to:", type in the name of an existing file and press ENTER. If the filename you enter cannot be found, the file is created for you by WordPerfect.

► ASCII FILES

See DOS (ASCII) TEXT FILES

ATTRIBUTE CHANGE

See APPEARANCE and SIZE for a change on the printed page; *see* COLORS/FONTS/ATTRIBUTES for a change on screen

AUTOMATICALLY FORMAT AND REWRITE

In Document

SCREEN (CTRL+F3) key
Rewrite (3 or R)

Manually readjusts text on screen according to current format settings (such as margins) after text is edited, which is useful if "Automatically Format and Rewrite" in Setup is set to No.

In Setup

SETUP (SHIFT+F1) key
Display (2 or D)
Edit Screen Options (6 or E)
Automatically Format and Rewrite (1 or A)
Y or N

Determines whether the WordPerfect program automatically reformats the document after you edit text or after you scroll completely through the text. If set to Yes (the default setting), simply press the down arrow key to reformat a document.

Type **Y** to set the automatic format or rewrite to Yes; type **N** to set it to No. If set to No, the down arrow key reformats only the next line; you must then reformat the document manually by moving the cursor or using the SCREEN key. It may be useful to turn Automatically Rewrite to No when you are working with complicated formatting, such as text columns.

▶ AUXILIARY FILES

See LOCATION OF FILES

▶ BACKUP

Drive Directory Location

Determines where timed backup files are stored on disk (see LOCATION OF FILES).

Timed

    SETUP (SHIFT+F1) key
    Environment (3 or E)
    Backup (1 or B)
    Timed Document Backup (1 or T)
    Y or N

Safeguards against the loss of text from the document on screen because of a power or machine failure. Text on the Doc 1 Typing screen is stored at the time interval specified in a file named WP{WP}.BK1, while text on the Doc 2 Typing screen is stored in WP{WP}.BK2. Thereafter, a document is saved at the time interval specified only if it is modified.

Type **Y** to turn the Timed Backup feature on, in which case
you must also enter a time interval representing the number
of minutes between each backup. Type **N** to turn the feature
off. If you turn the feature on and experience a power or
machine failure, restart WordPerfect, retrieve the backup file,
and resave it under a new filename. Also, after restarting,
WordPerfect will prompt at the time interval specified
whether you wish to rename or delete the already-existing
timed backup file.

Original

SETUP (SHIFT+F1) key
Environment (3 or E)
Backup (1 or B)
Original Document Backup (2 or O)
Y or N

Safeguards against accidentally replacing an original file on
disk with the document on your screen. As you edit a document on screen and resave it using the same filename, Word-
Perfect prompts "Replace?"; if you type **Y** to replace, the
document on screen is saved under the same filename, while
the original document on disk is renamed with the same
filename but with the .BK! extension.

Type **Y** to turn the Original Backup feature on; type **N** to
turn the feature off. If you turn the feature on and then
inadvertently replace an original file, you can retrieve and
rename the file with the .BK! extension.

▶ BASE FONT

See FONT

▶ BASELINE PLACEMENT FOR TYPESETTERS

FORMAT (SHIFT+F8) key
Other (4 or O)
Printer Functions (6 or P)
Baseline Placement for Typesetters (5 or B)
Y or N

Allows you to set the baseline (the bottom of the first line of text) even with the top margin. This ensures that the baseline will remain constant despite possible font changes in the text. Normally, the top of the first line of text is placed even with the top margin, so that the baseline is somewhat below the top margin. Baseline Placement has an effect only if you previously set Line Height to a fixed measurement (see LINE HEIGHT).

Type **Y** to set the first baseline on the page even with the top margin, or type **N** to turn off the feature and return to the normal setting.

► BEEP OPTIONS

SETUP (SHIFT+F1) key
Environment (3 or E)
Beep Options (2 or E)
Beep on Error (1 or E), Beep on Hyphenation (2 or Y),
    or Beep on Search Failure (3 or S)
Y or N

Determines whether or not the computer sounds a beep in three distinct situations: 1) when an error message appears on the status line, 2) when a request for a hyphenation decision appears on the status line, or 3) when a "*Not Found*" message appears on the status line after a search.

Type **Y** to have the computer beep, or type **N** to have the computer remain silent.

► BINDING OFFSET

PRINT (SHIFT+F7) key
Binding Offset (B)

A print option that can set an extra-wide margin on alternating pages for a document that you plan to bind like a book. The binding offset is set from the left edge (on odd-numbered pages) or the right edge (on even-numbered pages) of the page.

Enter a specific measurement. The binding offset is changed for every print job until you either change it or exit WordPerfect.

► BLOCK

Position cursor at one end of the text
BLOCK (ALT+F4) key
Position cursor at the opposite end of the text

Marks off (highlights) a portion of a document on which various commands can be performed. The cursor must be on the first or last character in the text before you press BLOCK. When you press BLOCK, the message "Block on" flashes on the screen. You can then use the cursor movement keys or the Search feature to move the cursor to the opposite end of the block, or if you are moving the cursor forward, you also can type a character to move to that character. (See also MOUSE for the procedure to block text using a mouse.) The text in the block becomes highlighted in reverse video.

The following features can then be used on the blocked text:

Appearance	Protect
Append	Replace
Bold	Save
Case Conversion	Search
Center	Size
Comment	Sort
Delete	Spell
Flush Right	Style
Mark Text	Table
Move /Copy	Underline
Print	

(Using Append, Delete, and Move/Copy, you can work not only with the standard highlighted block but also with a tabular column or a rectangle defined by that block.)

► BOLD

Using the Bold Key

BOLD (F6) key

Produces characters that are boldface (darker than normal) when printed. On screen, the bold text will display in a different color or brightness to distinguish it from normal text (see also COLORS/FONTS/ATTRIBUTES to set the way that the bold attribute is displayed on screen).

To activate boldface as you type, press BOLD (F6), type the text, and then press BOLD (F6) a second time, or press the right arrow key to turn off boldface. (The BOLD key is like a toggle switch; it turns boldface on if it was off or vice versa.)

To activate boldface for existing text, use the Block feature to highlight the existing text before pressing BOLD (F6).

Using the Font Key

Allows a second method for bolding characters (see AP-PEARANCE).

► BOXES

See GRAPHICS BOXES

▶ CALCULATE

See MATH COLUMNS and TABLES

▶ CANCEL

CANCEL (F1) key

Has various functions, depending on the status of the screen:
1) stops a macro or merge if one is in process, 2) clears a menu
or prompt that is on the screen, or 3) activates the Undelete
feature (see UNDELETE).

The Cancel feature can also be invoked if you have a
mouse by clicking the middle mouse button or clicking the
left and right mouse buttons simultaneously.

▶ CANCEL A PRINT JOB

See CONTROL PRINTER

▶ CAPITALIZATION

CAPS LOCK

Produces characters that are all in uppercase on screen and
when printed. CAPS LOCK affects only the letters A to Z.

To activate capitalization as you type, press CAPS LOCK,
type the text, and then press CAPS LOCK a second time to turn
off capitalization. (The CAPS LOCK key is like a toggle switch;
it turns capitalization on if it was off or vice versa.) When

CAPS LOCK is activated, the letters you type while pressing SHIFT appear in lowercase rather than uppercase. (To activate capitalization for existing text, see CASE CONVERSION.)

▶ CARTRIDGES AND FONTS

> PRINT (SHIFT+F7) key
> Select Printer (S)
> Position cursor on a printer name
> Edit (3 or E)
> Cartridges and Fonts (4 or C)
> Position cursor on font category of your choice
> Select (1 or S) or Change Quantity (2 or Q)

Defines additional cartridges, soft fonts, or print wheels that you have available for use with your printer.

When choosing the Select Fonts menu item, mark the cartridges or fonts that are listed in one of two ways: 1) with an asterisk (*) for Initially Present, indicating that the cartridge will be in a slot or in the printer memory when the print job begins (see also DOWNLOADABLE (SOFT) FONTS), or 2) with a plus sign (+) for Loaded During Print Job, indicating that you want WordPerfect to prompt you to insert (or remove) the cartridge or to load (or unload) the font during the print job, in which case the fonts and cartridges are returned to their original positions at the end of the print job. The fonts on the cartridges or downloadable files that you marked will now appear on the Base Font menu (see FONT).

► CASE CONVERSION

Block the text
SWITCH (SHIFT+F3) key
Uppercase (1 or U) or Lowercase (2 or L)

Switches a highlighted block of text to all uppercase or to all lowercase letters. When you switch to lowercase, the first character of a sentence remains in uppercase if the punctuation from the preceding sentence is included in the highlighted block.

► CENTER

CENTER (SHIFT+F6) key

Centers a short line of text between the left and right margins. (If you press TAB to tab over to a tab stop and then press CENTER, text is centered on the tab stop.)

To center text as you type, press CENTER (SHIFT+F6), type the text, and then press ENTER to move down to a new line.

To center existing text, position the cursor on the first character, press CENTER (SHIFT+F6), and then press the down arrow key. If you first use the Block feature to highlight a section of text and then press CENTER, numerous lines can be centered all at once (see also JUSTIFICATION).

Press CENTER twice in a row to precede text with dot leaders (. . . .).

► CENTER PAGE TOP TO BOTTOM

Position cursor at top of page
FORMAT (SHIFT+F8) key
Page (2 or P)
Center Page top to bottom (1 or C)
Y or N

Centers one page of text vertically between the top and the bottom of the page. Useful to center the text of a title page or a short letter.

Type **Y** to center the page or **N** to abort the command. The cursor must be positioned at the very beginning of a page, before any codes. The result takes effect at the printer, and is not shown on the Typing screen.

► CHANGE DRIVE/DIRECTORY

See DEFAULT DRIVE/DIRECTORY, CHANGE

► CLEAR DOCUMENT FROM SCREEN

EXIT (F7) key
Y to save document (in which case you must indicate a
    filename) or N to clear document without saving
Y to exit WordPerfect or N to remain in WordPerfect
    on a clear Typing screen

Clears the document currently on screen so that you can 1) begin typing a brand new document, 2) retrieve an existing document to the screen, or 3) exit WordPerfect.

If both the Doc 1 and Doc 2 Typing screens contain text (see WINDOWS), then instead of the last step listed in the key sequence, substitute the following:

> Y to exit the current Doc screen or N to remain on the current Doc screen

► CODES

See REVEAL CODES

► COLORS/FONTS/ATTRIBUTES

SETUP (SHIFT+F1) key
Display (2 or D)
Colors/Fonts/Attributes (1 or C)

Changes the way normal text, blocked (highlighted) text, and text with appearance or style attributes are displayed on the Typing screen. The options available to you, and thus the procedures for setting the on-screen display, depend on your display card and monitor.

If your monitor has font capabilities, you must select a set of fonts (such as italics or underline or 512 characters), and then you must select Screen Attributes or Screen Colors (1 or S) to assign a screen font color and/or other characteristics to each attribute listed. If you have a CGA monitor, you will be asked about the speed of writing text on screen, and then you must select Screen Colors (1 or S) to assign a screen color to each attribute listed. If you have a monochrome monitor, assign characteristics to each attribute listed.

After setting the on-screen display for one Typing screen (Doc 1 or Doc 2), press SWITCH (SHIFT+F3) to set the display for the other screen. You can copy the colors, fonts, and attribute settings from the Doc 1 screen to the Doc 2 screen with the MOVE (CTRL+F4) key.

► COLORS, PRINT

FONT (CTRL+F8) key
Print Color (5 or C)
Black (1 or K), White (2 or W), Red (3 or R), Green (4 or G), Blue (5 or B), Yellow (6 or Y), Magenta (7 or M), Cyan (8 or C), Orange (9 or E), Gray (A), Brown (N), or Other (O)

Providing that you have a color printer, sets the color for text on the printed page. Eleven colors are predefined (not all may be available with your printer). If you select the Other menu item, you could create a print color of your own design; enter a new intensity percentage for red, green, and blue.

To cancel the Print Color feature later in the text, reposition the cursor and repeat the same key sequence as when you turned on the color, except choose Black (1 or K) as the new color.

The color in which the text prints is independent of the on-screen color of text (see the COLORS/FONTS/ATTRI-BUTES section to set the on-screen color of text).

► COLUMNS, MATH

See MATH COLUMNS

► COLUMNS, TABULAR

See TABS to set or use tab stops for creating tabular columns; see also APPEND, DELETE, and MOVE/COPY

► COLUMNS, TEXT

See TEXT COLUMNS

► COMMENTS

Create

TEXT IN/OUT (CTRL+F5) key
Comment (4 or C)
Create (1 or C)

Creates a document comment in a double-line box, which is displayed on the screen but not when the document is printed. A comment is useful when you wish to insert a reminder for you or someone else who will work with that document.

Besides typing text into a comment, you can create a comment from existing text. Instead of following the key sequence just shown, use the Block feature to highlight the existing text, press TEXT IN/OUT (CTRL+F5), and then type **Y** to create a comment.

Convert to Text

> Position cursor below the comment
> TEXT IN/OUT (CTRL+F5) key
> Comment (4 or C)
> Convert to Text (3 or T)

Transforms the content of a comment into regular text so that it can be edited and printed as part of the document.

Edit

> TEXT IN/OUT (CTRL+F5) key
> Comment (4 or C)
> Edit (2 or E)

Edits the contents of a comment. WordPerfect first searches backwards to find the comment, so if your document contains more than one comment, position the cursor just forward from the comment you wish to edit before pressing TEXT IN/OUT.

Display

> SETUP (SHIFT+F1) key
> Display (2 or D)
> Edit Screen Options (6 or E)
> Comments Document (2 or D)
> Y or N

Specifies whether you wish to display all comments on screen or to hide them from view.

Type **Y** to display document comments, or type **N** to hide the display of comments on screen.

► COMPARE DOCUMENTS

See DOCUMENT COMPARE

► COMPOSE

> CTRL+2 or CTRL+V key
> Enter the WordPerfect character number

Inserts any special character into your document on screen, including multinational, box drawing, typographic, iconic, math/scientific, Greek, Hebrew, Cyrillic, and Japanese kana symbols. Be aware that certain monitors cannot display specific special characters, and certain non-graphics printers cannot print specific special characters.

Before inserting a special character, look up its Word-Perfect character number in the document named CHAR-ACTR.DOC (which resides on your hard disk or the Install/Utility floppy disk). A WordPerfect character number is composed of a character set number, a comma, and a character number from within the set, such as 3,9 or 4,17.

You can use CTRL+V only when viewing the Typing or Reveal Codes screen, while CTRL+2 can also be used when viewing a menu. CTRL+V causes WordPerfect to display the prompt "Key =". CTRL+2 causes no prompt to display. (See DIGRAPHS/DIACRITICAL MARKS and KEYBOARD LAYOUT.)

4,11 = £.

► CONCORDANCE

See INDEXES

► CONDITIONAL END OF PAGE

FORMAT (SHIFT+F8) key
Other (4 or O)
Conditional End of Page (2 or C)

Ensures that a block of lines remains undivided by a soft page break. This is useful to keep a heading together with its accompanying text.

Position the cursor on the line before the text you wish to keep together before starting the key sequence. When Word-Perfect prompts "Number of Lines to Keep Together:", type in the number of lines and press ENTER. Beginning with the next line, that number of lines will stay on the same page. (For other ways to control page breaks, see also PROTECT, BLOCK, PAGE BREAKS, and WIDOW/ORPHAN PROTECTION.)

► CONTROL PRINTER

PRINT (SHIFT+F7) key
Control Printer (4 or C)
Cancel Job(s) (1 or C), Rush Job (2 or R), Display Jobs
    (3 or D), Go (4 or G), or Stop (5 or S)

Manages the print jobs that are waiting in line to be printed, using the following options:

- Cancel Job(s): Removes one or all print jobs from the print queue.

- Display Jobs: Displays all print jobs, which is useful if there are more than three print jobs, the maximum that can be displayed on the Control Printer Screen.

- Go (start printer): Resumes printing after a pause to insert a new print wheel, to manually feed paper, or after stopping a print job.

- Rush Job: Rearranges the order of print jobs in the print queue, moving a specified job to the top of the list.

- Stop: Stops the printer (without removing a job from the print queue) until you type **G** to resume printing or **C** to cancel the print job.

► CONVERT FILES TO/FROM WORDPERFECT

Exit WordPerfect to DOS
Type **CONVERT**

Executes the CONVERT.EXE file, which is housed on your hard disk or on the Install/Utility floppy disk. This file transfers files from any of the following formats into WordPerfect version 5.1: WordStar, MultiMate, Word, Revisable-Form-Text and Final-Form-Text (intermediary for IBM products like DisplayWrite), Navy DIF, MailMerge (WordStar and dBASE, among others), Spreadsheet DIF, and WordPerfect version 4.2. Also transfers WordPerfect files into these other formats and translates a WordPerfect file into seven-bit or eight-bit format for sending a WordPerfect document over a modem.

When WordPerfect prompts, you must enter the name of the file to be converted (the input file); include the location where the file is located if it is different from the default drive or directory. Also, you must enter the name of the file to be created (the output file). Then indicate the type of conversion you desire from the menu that is displayed.

(See also DOS (ASCII) TEXT FILES, SAVE, and SPREADSHEET for additional procedures in transferring files to and from WordPerfect format.)

▶ COPY FILES

KEY SEQUENCE:

LIST (F5) key
Type drive or directory name and press ENTER
Position cursor on a file
Copy (8 or C)
Type drive or directory name and press ENTER

Places a second copy of the file into a new drive or directory. This is useful when you wish to back up files as a safety precaution or if you wish to reorganize files on disk.

You can copy two or more files in one command by marking the files you wish to copy with an asterisk before selecting Copy (see MARK FILES).

► COPY TEXT

See MOVE/COPY

► CROSS-REFERENCE

Mark Reference and Target

Position cursor in the referring text
MARK TEXT (ALT+F5) key
Cross-Ref (1 or R)
Mark Both Reference and Target (3 or B)
Page Number (1 or P), Paragraph/Outline Number (2 or
   O), Footnote Number (3 or F), Endnote Number (4 or
   E), or Graphics Box Number (5 or G); this
   specifies the type of target
Position cursor to location immediately following
   target and press ENTER
Enter target name

Creates a reference to a specific graphics box, page paragraph/outline, footnote, or endnote number. For example, the reference may be "Refer to page 44," where the target is page 44. The reference and target are marked in the same key sequence.

When WordPerfect prompts "Target Name:", indicate a name that ties the reference and target. The reference code (and thus the position of the cursor when you begin the key sequence) can be placed in regular text, a header, a footer, a footnote, an endnote, a graphics box caption, or a graphics text box. A target code can be placed in regular text on a page, next to a paragraph/outline number, in a footnote, in an endnote, or in a graphics box caption.

Mark Reference Only

Position cursor in the referring text
MARK TEXT (ALT+F5) key
Cross-Ref (1 or R)
Mark Reference (1 or R)
Page Number (1 or P), Paragraph/Outline Number (2 or O), Footnote Number (3 or F), Endnote Number (4 or E), or Graphics Box Number (5 or G); this specifies the type of target
Enter target name

Useful if you wish to mark the reference and target separately or if you wish to create multiple references to the same target. A question mark appears in place of the reference number, such as "Refer to Page ?". After you mark the target in a separate operation, you must then update the cross-reference (see *Update*).

When WordPerfect prompts "Target Name:", indicate a name that will be also used for the target. The reference code (and thus the position of the cursor when you begin the key sequence) can be placed in regular text, a header, a footer, a footnote, an endnote, a graphics box caption, or a graphics text box.

Market Target Only

Position cursor to location immediately following target
MARK TEXT (ALT+F5) key
Cross-Ref (1 or R)

Mark Target (2 or T)
Enter target name

Useful if you wish to mark the reference and target separately or if you wish to create multiple targets for a single reference. After you mark the target in a separate operation, you must then update the cross-reference (see *Update*).

When WordPerfect prompts "Target Name:", indicate a name that has also been used for the reference. A target code can be placed in regular text on a page, next to a paragraph/outline number, in a footnote, in an endnote, or in a graphics box caption.

Update

Updates the cross-references in a document, which is necessary if you 1) marked the reference and target separately or 2) edited the text after marking the references and targets, so that the references must be revised (see GENERATE CROSS-REFERENCES, ENDNOTES, INDEXES, LISTS, TABLES for the key sequence).

► CURSOR MOVEMENT KEYS

See the General Reminders section

► CURSOR SPEED

SETUP (SHIFT+F1) key
Environment (3 or E)
Cursor Speed (3 or C)

Increases or decreases the speed with which keys repeat on the keyboard when they are held down. By default, Word-Perfect is set to repeat 50 times for every second a key is held down. Other options include 15, 20, 30, or 40 characters per second, as well as Normal, which returns your keyboard to its normal cursor speed and avoids potential incompatibilities with Terminate and Stay Resident programs.

▶ DATE (AND TIME)

Code

> DATE/OUTLINE (SHIFT+F5) key
> Date Code (2 or C)

Inserts the date and/or time on screen as a hidden code in the current date format. The date or time will be updated whenever you retrieve or print that document. To use this feature correctly, be sure that the computer clock has been set.

Format

> DATE/OUTLINE (SHIFT+F5) key
> Date Format (3 or F)

Specifies the way the date and/or time are displayed when you choose to insert the date (either as text or as a code) using the DATE/OUTLINE key. Text, numbers, and punctuation can be included in the date format. This format stays in effect for the entire working session or until you again change the date format. The default date format is Month ##, 19##, which can be permanently altered from the Initial Settings menu (see INITIAL SETTINGS).

Text

DATE/OUTLINE (SHIFT+F5) key
Date Text (1 or T)

Inserts the date and/or time on the screen as text in the current date format. To use this feature correctly, be sure that the computer's clock has been set.

▶ DECIMAL/ALIGN CHARACTER

FORMAT (SHIFT+F8) key
Other (4 or O)
Decimal/Align Character (3 or D)

Alters the character used with the Tab Align, Tabs, and Math features to align numbers (see also TAB ALIGN, TABS, and MATH COLUMNS). After entering a decimal/align character, you can also enter a thousands' separator (see also THOUSANDS' SEPARATOR).

▶ DEFAULT DOCUMENT TYPE

SETUP (SHIFT+F1) key
Environment (3 or E)
Document Management/Summary (4 or D)
Default Document Type (4 or T)

Establishes a long document type, such as "In-house memo" or "Letter," that will be assumed whenever the Long Document Names feature is activated and WordPerfect prompts for a document type (see also LONG DOCUMENT NAMES). A document type can contain up to 20 characters.

DEFAULT DRIVE/DIRECTORY, CHANGE

LIST (F5) key
=
Enter drive or directory name

or

LIST (F5) key
ENTER
Other directory (7 or O)
Enter drive or directory name

Changes the default for where WordPerfect assumes you wish to save files to and retrieve files from for the entire working session or until you change the default again. Indicate a specific disk drive by typing the appropriate drive letter followed by a colon, such as A:, B:, or C:. Indicate a directory on the hard disk (C:) by preceding each directory level with a backslash, as in C:\WP51, C:\WP51\DATA, or C:\WP51\BUD. (See also LOCATION OF FILES for the procedure to establish the same default drive/directory at the start of each working session.)

▶ DEFAULT SETTINGS, CHANGE

See INITIAL SETTINGS

▶ DELETE A CODE

Erases a code from the screen, thus aborting the effect of a feature that was activated by initially inserting that code. Locate a code that you wish to delete using either the Reveal Codes or Search feature (see these separate entries), and then delete the code using the DELETE or BACKSPACE key. You can also use the Macro or Replace feature (see these separate entries) to delete all occurrences of a given code in a document.

▶ DELETE FILES

LIST (F5) key
Type drive or directory name and press ENTER
Position cursor on file
Delete (2 or D)
Y to confirm

Deletes a file from disk, which is useful when the file is obsolete and you wish to free up room on disk.

You can delete two or more files in one command by marking the files you wish to delete with an asterisk before selecting Delete (see MARK FILES).

DELETE TEXT

Block, Tabular Column, or Rectangle

Block the text
MOVE (CTRL+F4) key
Block (1 or B), Tabular Column (2 or C), or Rectangle
  (3 or R)
Delete (3 or D)

Deletes a block. The block can highlight not only a standard cluster of text, but also a tabular column or rectangle. To highlight a tabular column, which is text or numbers aligned on a tab stop, position the cursor on any character in the first line of the column, press BLOCK (ALT+F4), and then position the cursor on any character in the last line of the column. When you press the Tabular Column menu item, only that one column will be highlighted. To highlight a rectangle, position the cursor on the character that represents the upper-left corner of the rectangle, press BLOCK (ALT+F4), and then use the cursor to highlight up to the character that represents the lower-right corner of the rectangle. When you press the Rectangle menu item, only the text that comprises that rectangle will be highlighted.

Character(s), Word(s), Line(s)

See the General Reminders section

Sentence, Paragraph, or Page

Position cursor within the sentence, paragraph, or page
MOVE (CTRL+F4) key
Sentence (1 or S), Paragraph (2 or P), or Page (3 or A)
Delete (3 or D)

Deletes the highlighted sentence, paragraph, or page.

▶ DICTIONARY

See SPELLER

▶ DIGRAPHS/DIACRITICAL MARKS

CTRL+2 or CTRL+V key
Type a character
Type a second character or a symbol

Inserts into your document on screen either a digraph, which is two vowels or consonants combined to express one sound (such as æ), or a diacritical mark, which is a vowel or consonant combined with a symbol to express one sound (such as ñ). This feature is useful to circumvent having to look up a digraph or diacritical mark's WordPerfect character number. Be aware that certain monitors cannot display specific digraphs or diacritical marks, and certain (non-graphics) printers cannot print specific ones.

When viewing the Typing or Reveal Codes screen, you can use CTRL+2 or CTRL+V. When viewing a menu, only CTRL+V operates. CTRL+V causes WordPerfect to display the prompt "Key =". CTRL+2 does not display a prompt. (See also COMPOSE and KEYBOARD LAYOUT.)

▶ DIRECTORY

Change Default

See DEFAULT DRIVE/DIRECTORY, CHANGE

Create

LIST (F5) key
=
Enter new directory
Y to confirm

or

LIST (F5) key
ENTER
Other Directory (7 or O)
Enter new directory
Y to confirm

Creates a new directory and is most useful for hard disk users who create directories as a way of organizing files on disk.

Delete

LIST (F5) key
Type name of parent directory and press ENTER
Position cursor on subdirectory name
Delete (2 or D)
Y to confirm

Erases a directory from disk. This can only be accomplished when the directory contains no files. Also, a list of files for the parent of the directory you wish to delete must be displayed.

► DISPLAY

SETUP (SHIFT+F1) key
Display (2 or D)

Alters the defaults for the screen display, including the following features:

- Colors/Fonts/Attributes: Determines how text with various attributes appears on screen (see this separate entry).

- Graphics/Text Screen Type: Selects a graphics driver for your graphics card and monitor, and a text driver for when you are in Text mode. (Usually, WordPerfect selects the correct graphics and text drivers automatically.)

- Menu Options: Determines how various menus display on screen, including how mnemonic letters are denoted in function key menus (you can select most menu items by pressing either their corresponding number or mnemonic letter); how mnemonic letters and how other text is denoted in pull-down menus and on the pull-down menu bar; and whether a double separator line appears below the menu bar. You can also specify whether the ALT key alone (rather than ALT+=) activates the

pull-down menus, and whether the menu bar
remains at the top of the Typing screen at all times.

- View Document Options: Indicates whether, on the
  View Document screen, color monitors display text
  in black and white, graphics in black and white, and
  bold characters as brighter characters or in color.

- Edit-Screen Options: Determines how the Typing
  screen appears and operates as you type and edit
  your text, including whether WordPerfect rewrites
  the screen as you edit or instead as you scroll
  through the text (see AUTOMATICALLY
  FORMAT AND REWRITE); whether document
  comments are displayed or hidden from view;
  whether a document's filename is displayed in the
  lower-left corner on the status line after the first time
  you save that document; what character, if any, is
  used to indicate a hard return [HRt] on the Typing
  screen; whether Merge codes are displayed on the
  Typing screen; the size of the bottom section on the
  Reveal Codes screen; and whether text formatted
  into columns is displayed side-by-side or on separate
  pages on screen (see also TEXT COLUMNS).

▶ DISPLAY PITCH

FORMAT (SHIFT+F8) key
Document (3 or D)
Display Pitch (1 or D)

Sets the amount of horizontal space that one character occupies on screen. Decreasing the pitch expands the document horizontally. Useful for altering text on screen when text is formatted into columns or when using tabs and indents, where text appears to overlap on screen.

Type **Y** to have WordPerfect adjust the pitch automatically, or type **N** to enter a display pitch of your own. Then enter a display pitch width. When the display pitch is automatic, it can be decreased but not increased.

► DOCUMENT COMMENTS

See COMMENTS

► DOCUMENT COMPARE

MARK TEXT (ALT+F5) key
Generate (6 or G)
Compare Screen and Disk Documents (2 or C)

Compares a document on the screen to a document on disk and is useful after you have edited a contract or other document and wish to compare the original with the revision. WordPerfect compares the documents phrase-by-phrase, where a phrase is defined as text between punctuation marks. On-screen text that does not exist in the file on disk is redlined. Text in the file on disk that does not exist in the document on the screen is copied to the on-screen document with strikeout codes inserted. (See also REDLINE and STRIKEOUT.) For a section of text that is moved, WordPerfect inserts "The

Following Text Was Moved" before the text and "The Preceding Text Was Moved" after the text.

When WordPerfect prompts with "Other Document:", it suggests a filename of the original document on disk. Press ENTER to accept that filename, or enter another filename. (See also REMOVE REDLINE AND STRIKEOUT for the method to return the on-screen document to its edited version.)

► DOCUMENT FORMAT

See FORMAT

► DOCUMENT INITIAL CODES

See INITIAL CODES

► DOCUMENT MANAGEMENT/SUMMARY

SETUP (SHIFT+F1)
Environment (3 or E)
Document Management/Summary (4 or D)

Specifies options for managing documents, including whether a document summary form appears automatically the first time you save a document (see Display Automatically in SUMMARY), the default text for a subject search (see Subject Search Text in SUMMARY), whether to name a document with a short or with a long document name (see LONG

DOCUMENT NAMES), and the default document type (see DEFAULT DOCUMENT TYPE).

▶ DOCUMENT SUMMARY

See SUMMARY

▶ DOS, EXIT TO

SHELL (CTRL+F1) key
Go to DOS (1 or G) or DOS Command (2 or C)

Exits temporarily to DOS so that you can type DOS commands as desired. Select Go to DOS in order to execute many commands; when you wish to return to WordPerfect, type the word **EXIT** and press ENTER at the DOS prompt. (If you run WordPerfect under Shell, you must first temporarily exit to Shell and then go to DOS.) Or, select DOS Command to execute a single DOS command; afterwards, press any key to resume in WordPerfect.

▶ DOS (ASCII) TEXT FILES

Save as DOS Text File

TEXT IN/OUT (CTRL+F5) key
DOS Text (1 or T)
Save (1 or S)

Stores a file on disk as a DOS (ASCII) text file, stripping it of any special formatting codes so that that file can then be used from DOS or transferred for use in another software package. It is also useful when you wish to save a DOS batch file to disk. (See also the section for generic word processing in SAVE.)

Retrieve a DOS Text File

TEXT IN/OUT (CTRL+F5) key
DOS Text (1 or T)
Retrieve CR/LF to [HRt] (2 or R) or Retrieve CR/LF
    to [SRt] (3 or E)

Retrieves a DOS (ASCII) text file to the screen. Useful once a file has been converted from another software program to a DOS text file, or if you wish to retrieve and then edit a DOS batch file already on disk.

Retrieve CR/LF to [SRt], the third menu item on the DOS Text menu, inserts a soft return [SRt] code rather than a hard return [HRt] code at the end of lines that fall within WordPerfect's Hyphenation Zone. The Retrieve CR/LF to [HRt] item on the DOS Text menu inserts a hard return [HRt] code at the end of every line.

▶ DOT LEADERS

See TABS, CENTER, and FLUSH RIGHT

► DOUBLE UNDERLINE

Underlines text with a double underscore at the printer (see APPEARANCE for the key sequence).

► DOWNLOADABLE (SOFT) FONTS

Define

Defines soft fonts that you have available for use with your printer as either Initially Present or Loaded During Print Job (see CARTRIDGES AND FONTS for the key sequence).

Download

PRINT (SHIFT+F7) key
Initialize Printer (7 or I)

Clears any soft fonts from the printer's memory and loads soft fonts defined as Initially Present.

Path

PRINT (SHIFT+F7) key
Select Printer (S)
Position cursor on a printer name
Edit (3 or E)
Path for Downloadable Font (6 or D)

Indicates the drive and directory where WordPerfect should look to find downloadable font files.

▶ DRAW LINES

See LINE DRAW or GRAPHICS LINES

▶ DUAL DOCUMENT TYPING

See WINDOWS

▶ EDITING KEYS

See the General Reminders section

▶ ENDNOTES

See FOOTNOTES/ENDNOTES

▶ ENTER KEY

See RETURN

▶ ENVELOPES AND LABELS

FORMAT (SHIFT+F8) key
Page (2 or P)
Paper Size/Type (7 or S)
Position cursor on Envelope or Labels paper definition
Select (1 or S)

Properly formats a document containing addresses for printing on envelopes or mailing labels.

For envelopes, make sure that you have defined a paper definition for envelopes (see PAPER DEFINITIONS). Also, make sure to alter margins for the new paper size. For envelopes with the return address preprinted, try the following margin settings (see MARGINS): left = 4.5", right = 0", top = 2.5", bottom = 0".

For mailing labels, make sure that you have defined a paper definition for labels (see PAPER DEFINITIONS).

▶ ENVIRONMENT

SETUP (SHIFT+F1) key
Environment (3 or E)

Alters settings that effect the working environment in WordPerfect, including Backup Options, Beep Options, Cursor Speed, Document Management/Summary, Fast Save, and Units of Measure (see these separate entries). In addition, you can specify two different aspects of how hyphenation operates after it is turned on (see HYPHENATION). First, you can indicate whether WordPerfect should hyphenate using the hyphenation program, contained in the file that is called WP{WP}US.HYC, or using internal rules. The hyphenation program is more accurate, but occupies additional disk space. Second, you can indicate whether WordPerfect always prompts you to determine a hyphen location, sometimes prompts, or never prompts. A change in the Environment menu remains in effect each time you start WordPerfect thereafter.

► EQUATIONS

Editor

Creates and edits a mathematical or scientific equation (see *Edit Contents* in GRAPHICS BOXES).

Initial Settings

> SETUP (SHIFT+F1)
> Initial Settings (4 or I)
> Equation (3 or E)

Determines default options for the Equation Editor, including whether the equation should print in Graphics or Text mode; the equation's font size on the printed page; the equation's horizontal and vertical alignments; and a keyboard definition, if any, used to aid in creating the equation. These options can be altered for a specific equation by pressing SETUP while in the Equation Editor.

► ERROR MESSAGES

Self-explanatory prompts that indicate the wrong key was pressed or a command that you wish to execute cannot be performed. Common error messages and solutions include the following:

- "Are Other Copies of WordPerfect Running?": Type **N** to reload WordPerfect if you experienced a power or machine failure or if you turned off the computer without exiting WordPerfect properly the last time

WordPerfect was running. Type **Y** and indicate a
different directory if you have sufficient memory
and wish to run two copies of WordPerfect at once.
This allows overflow files for the second copy to be
stored in that other directory.

- "Disk Full, Press Any Key to Continue": If you are
  attempting to save a file, delete some unwanted files
  on disk or insert another disk before you try again. If
  you are attempting to print, try printing from disk
  instead of from screen.

- "File Not Found": Try again to enter the proper
  filename or to indicate the proper drive or directory
  where the file is stored.

- "Insufficient File Handles to Run WordPerfect":
  Include the FILES=20 command that must be
  present in the CONFIG.SYS file to run WordPerfect.
  Then restart your computer.

- "Not Enough Memory": If your document is large,
  split it into smaller files. If text is contained in both
  the Doc 1 and Doc 2 windows, erase the text from
  one of the windows. You may want to purchase
  more memory for your computer.

- "WP Disk Full, Press Any Key to Continue":
  Redirect overflow files to the data disk using the /D
  start-up option (see START-UP OPTIONS).
  Consider purchasing more memory or a hard disk
  for your computer.

► ESCAPE KEY

See REPEAT VALUE

► EXIT

EXIT (F7) key
Y to save document (in which case you must indicate a
    filename) or N to clear document without saving
Y to exit WordPerfect

Allows you to exit WordPerfect so that you can load another
software package or turn off the computer. Always exit Word-
Perfect at the end of a WordPerfect working session before
you turn off your computer.

If both the Doc 1 and Doc 2 Typing screens contain text
(see WINDOWS), the key sequence just shown exits one of
the Doc screens instead of exiting WordPerfect. Repeat the
key sequence a second time to exit WordPerfect.

► EXTENDED CHARACTERS

See COMPOSE

► EXTRA LARGE

Prints text in extra-large-size characters for the base font (see
SIZE for the key sequence).

▶ FAST SAVE

SETUP (SHIFT+F1) key
Environment (3 or E)
Fast Save unformatted (5 or F)
Y or N

Directs WordPerfect to save files without formatting before doing so. This speeds up the time it takes to save a document. However, it will take longer to print an unformatted document from disk, because the document must be formatted first.

Type **Y** to activate the Fast Save feature, or type **N** to turn off the feature.

▶ FILE MANAGEMENT

See COPY, DELETE, DIRECTORY, FIND, LOOK, MOVE/RENAME, NAME SEARCH, PRINT, RETRIEVE, SAVE, SHORT/LONG DISPLAY and SUMMARY.

▶ FILENAME ON STATUS LINE

See DISPLAY

▶ FIND FILES

LIST (F5) key
Type drive or directory name and press ENTER
Find (9 or F)

Name (1 or N), Doc Summary (2 or D), First Page
(3 or P), Entire Doc (4 or E), Conditions (5 or C),
or Undo (6 or U)

Rewrites the List Files screen, displaying only those files that
meet certain conditions. The conditions you can specify include 1) a certain word pattern (one or more words) in a
document summary, 2) a certain word pattern in the
document's first page of text, 3) a certain word pattern anywhere within the document, 4) a certain date when the file
was last saved on disk, 5) any combination of those conditions, or 6) a certain character pattern in the file's name, such
as "LT", which would find the files LT059, JONES.LTR, and
ALTMAN. Use this to find a file or group of files on a specific
drive or in a specific directory.

The word pattern can contain one or more words. For two
words separated by a comma, WordPerfect searches for documents that contain either word. For two words separated by
a space or semicolon (;), WordPerfect searches for documents
that contain both words. For words within quotation marks,
WordPerfect searches for documents that contain that exact
phrase of words.

For the Doc Summary, First Page, or Entire Doc menu
item, type in the word pattern you wish to search on. For the
Conditions menu item, a Word Search screen appears so you
can specify more than one search condition; after specifying
the conditions, select the Perform Search On menu item to
begin the search, or select the Undo menu item to undo the
current search conditions.

You can search on only selected files by marking them
with an asterisk before selecting Find (see MARK FILES).

▶ FINE

Prints text in fine (the smallest) size for the base font (see SIZE for the key sequence).

▶ FLUSH RIGHT

FLUSH RIGHT (ALT+F6) key

Places a short line of text flush against the right margin and is useful to align dates or memorandum headings.

To make text flush right as you type, press FLUSH RIGHT (ALT+F6), type the text, and then press ENTER to move down to a new line.

To flush right existing text, position the cursor on the first character, press FLUSH RIGHT (ALT+F6), and then press the down arrow key. If you first use the Block feature to highlight a section of text and then press FLUSH RIGHT, numerous lines can be aligned flush right all at once (see also JUSTIFICATION).

Press FLUSH RIGHT twice in a row to precede the text with dot leaders (. . . .).

▶ FONT

Attributes

On the printed page, alters the text's appearance or size for the base font (see APPEARANCE and SIZE).

Base

FONT (CTRL+F8) key
Base Font (4 or F)
Position cursor on font of your choice
Select (1 or S)

Alters the font for regular text in a particular section of a document. When a document is first created, the base font is set as whatever has been established as the *initial* base font for that document.

Position the cursor anywhere within the document to alter the base font starting at that location.

Downloadable

See DOWNLOADABLE (SOFT) FONTS

Initial Base (for a Specific Document)

FORMAT (SHIFT+F8) key
Document (3 or D)
Initial Base Font (3 or F)
Position cursor on font of your choice
Select (1 or S)

For a particular document, alters the font for all text—including regular text, headers, footers, footnotes, endnotes, and captions. When a document is first created, the initial base font for that document is assumed to be the same as the initial base font for whatever *printer* has been selected for that document.

Initial Base (for a Specific Printer)

PRINT (SHIFT+F7) key
Select Printer (S)
Position cursor on a printer name
Edit (3 or E)
Initial Base Font (5 or F)
Position cursor on font of your choice
Select (1 or S)

For a particular printer, alters the font used to print out all documents. Thereafter, whenever you select that printer for printing a document, the printer's initial base font is assumed unless it is altered. The fonts available for selection depend on your printer's built-in fonts and on the fonts you mark as available on printer cartridges or soft fonts (see CARTRIDGES AND FONTS).

Normal

FONT (CTRL+F8) key
Normal (3 or N)

Turns off all appearance and size attributes at one time so that text returns to normal for the base font.

► FOOTERS

See HEADERS/FOOTERS

► FOOTNOTES/ENDNOTES

Create

FOOTNOTE (CTRL+F7) key
Footnote (1 or F) or Endnote (2 or E)
Create (1 or C)

Inserts a note reference number in the main text, which will be superscripted when printed. The text of a footnote appears at the bottom of the same page as the note reference number. The text of an endnote appears at the end of the document unless you use the Endnote Placement feature (see *Endnote Placement*).

A footnote or endnote Typing screen appears, automatically displaying a note reference number. Type in the text of the note.

Edit

FOOTNOTE (CTRL+F7) key
Footnote (1 or F) or Endnote (2 or E)
Edit (2 or E)

Edits a previously created footnote or endnote.When Word-Perfect prompts "Footnote number?" or "Endnote number?", type in the note number and press ENTER. The note text appears on the screen for editing.

Endnote Placement

FOOTNOTE (CTRL+F7) key
Endnote Placement (3 or P)
Y or N to restart numbering

Specifies a location where all endnotes that have been created prior to that location should be printed. Endnotes created beyond that location will print at the end of the document (or at the next endnote placement location).

When WordPerfect prompts "Restart endnote numbering?", type **Y** if you want all endnotes that follow to begin again at number 1. Type **N** if you want to continue with consecutive numbering. WordPerfect marks the endnote placement location on the Typing screen by displaying the following comment in a single-line box: "Endnote Placement. It is not known how much space endnotes will occupy here. Generate to determine." (See *Generate Endnotes*.)

Generate Endnotes

Allows you to determine how much space endnotes will occupy wherever you inserted an Endnote Placement code in a document. (For the key sequence, see GENERATE CROSS-REFERENCES, ENDNOTES, INDEXES, LISTS, TABLES.) Once the endnotes are generated, the comment in a single-line box that marks the endnote placement location now reads "Endnote Placement". To determine the space that will be occupied by endnotes in the printed document, examine the line indicator ("Ln") on the status line as you position the cursor above and then below the comment.

New Note Number

FOOTNOTE (CTRL+F7) key
Footnote (1 or F) or Endnote (2 or E)
New Number (3 or N)

Renumbers all footnotes or endnotes beyond the cursor position. You must rewrite the screen by using the cursor movement keys or the Rewrite Screen feature for the new numbering to take effect.

When WordPerfect prompts "Footnote number?" or "Endnote number?", enter a new number.

Options

FOOTNOTE (CTRL+F7) key
Footnote (1 or F) or Endnote (2 or E)
Options (4 or O)

Alters any of the initial settings for how footnotes or endnotes will appear in a particular printed document, including the following:

- Spacing: The spacing (such as single or double spacing) within and between footnotes or endnotes.

- Keep Together: The amount of a footnote or endnote to keep together on one page if the note in its entirety cannot fit on one page, so that the second half must continue on the following page.

- Style: The style for the reference note number in the text of the document as well as in the footnote or endnote itself.

- Numbering Method: The symbol used to mark footnotes or endnotes. The options include numbers, letters, or characters such as * and #.

Also allows for changing additional initial settings for footnotes only, including the following:

- Start Numbers Each Page: Whether or not footnote numbering restarts at 1 after each page break.

- Separating Line: The line separating text from the footnotes.

- Continued Message: Whether or not a "(Continued)" message prints if a footnote must be split between two pages.

- Footnote at Bottom: Whether the footnote is printed at the bottom of the page or just below the text (in the event that the text does not occupy a full page).

► FORCE ODD/EVEN PAGE

FORMAT (SHIFT+F8) key
Page (2 or P)
Force Odd/Even Pages (2 or O)
Odd (1 or O) or Even (2 or E)

Forces the page number on the current page to be odd or even.

► FOREIGN LANGUAGES

See LANGUAGE

► FORMAT

FORMAT (SHIFT+F8) key
Line (1 or L), Page (2 or P), Document (3 or D), or
Other (4 or O)

Provides access to the four separate menus that insert format codes in a document to alter format settings. A format code affects a document beginning at the location of the code and continuing either to the next code of the same type or to the end of the document.

Position the cursor on the Document Initial Codes screen or at the top of the document to alter the format starting at the top. You also can position the cursor anywhere within the document to alter the format starting at that location.

For Line Format features, see HYPHENATION, JUSTI-FICATION, LINE HEIGHT, LINE NUMBERING, LINE SPACING, *Left/Right* in MARGINS, TABS, and WIDOW/ORPHAN PROTECTION.

For Page Format features, see CENTER TOP TO BOT-TOM, FORCE ODD/EVEN PAGE, HEADERS/FOOTERS, *Top/Bottom* in MARGINS, PAGE NUMBERING, PAPER SIZE/TYPE, and SUPPRESS.

For Document Format features, see DISPLAY PITCH, *Document* in INITIAL CODES, *Base* and *Initial* in FONT, REDLINE, and SUMMARY. These features take effect for the entire document, and no format code is inserted.

For Other Format features, see ADVANCE, CONDI-
TIONAL END OF PAGE, DECIMAL CHARACTER,
THOUSANDS' SEPARATOR, LANGUAGE, OVER-
STRIKE, PRINTER FUNCTIONS, and UNDERLINE
SPACES AND TABS.

► FORMS

See PAPER DEFINITIONS

► FUNCTION KEYS

Provides access to WordPerfect functions and features. See
the General Reminders section for a list of the key names
corresponding to each of the function keys. To display a list
of function key names in the form of a template, press HELP
(F3) twice. Press ENTER to return to your document.

► GENERATE CROSS-REFERENCES, ENDNOTES, INDEXES, LISTS, TABLES

MARK TEXT (ALT+F5) key
Generate (6 or G)
Generate Tables, Indexes, Cross-References, etc.
 (5 or G)
Y or N

Updates cross-references if you edit your text after you mark references and targets (see CROSS-REFERENCE). Also creates (or replaces) lists, tables, or an index once you have marked the text and defined the format for the lists, tables, or index (see LISTS, TABLES OF AUTHORITIES, TABLES OF CONTENTS, and INDEXES). Also determines how much space endnotes will occupy if you inserted an Endnote Placement code (see FOOTNOTES/ENDNOTES).

► GO TO

Swiftly moves the cursor to specific locations in a document or in text columns (see the General Reminders section).

► GO TO DOS

See DOS, EXIT TO

► GRAPHICS BOXES

Create

GRAPHICS (ALT+F9) key
Figure (1 or F), Table Box (2 or T), Text Box (3 or B),
    User Box (4 or U), or Equation (6 or E)
Create (1 or C)

Incorporates a box that contains either text, an equation, or an image into a document. The rest of the text in the document wraps around the box. You can select from five different box styles: figure, table, text, user-defined, or equation. Each style has a different set of default characteristics and is numbered separately from the other box styles.

WordPerfect displays a menu on which you define the box's characteristics, including 1) the filename (preceded with a drive or directory if different from the default) that contains text or a graphics image that you wish to place in the box, 2) the contents—either a graphics image, a graphics image as a separate file, text, or an equation, 3) the box caption, 4) the anchor type—either character, paragraph, or page —which determines how the box is positioned relative to text on the page, 5) the vertical position of the box, 6) the horizontal position of the box, 7) the size (width and height) of the box, 8) whether text wraps around the box, and 9) any editing required for the box's contents (see *Edit Contents*).

After a graphics box is created, a box outline, but not the box contents, appears on the Typing screen. The box contents appear on the printed page.

Edit Box Definition

GRAPHICS (ALT+F9) key
Figure (1 or F), Table Box (2 or T), Text Box (3 or B),
    User Box (4 or U), or Equation (6 or E)
Edit (2 or E)

Edits the definition of a previously created graphics box. When WordPerfect prompts, type in the number of the graphics box (of that particular style) that you wish to edit and press ENTER. On the menu that appears, you can redefine the box characteristics.

Edit Contents

GRAPHICS (ALT+F9) key
Figure (1 or F), Table Box (2 or T), Text Box (3 or B),
    User Box (4 or U), or Equation (6 or E)
Create (1 or C) or Edit (2 or E)
Edit (9 or E)

Edits the contents of a graphics box. How the Editor operates
depends on the box contents. If the box contents indicate
"text", use the Editor to type or edit the text. If the box contents
indicate "graphics image", use the Editor to move, scale,
rotate, or invert the image displayed on screen. If the box
contents indicate "equation", use the Editor to create and
format mathematical and scientific equations. The Equation
Editor is composed of three windows: the editing window,
where you type and edit the text of the equation; the equation
palette, from which you can select commands and special
symbols for insertion into the equation, and the display window, where the final result can be viewed. Use the LIST key
to choose items from the equation palette and the SWITCH key
to view the equation in the display window.

New Number

GRAPHICS (ALT+F9) key
Figure (1 or F), Table Box (2 or T), Text Box (3 or B),
    User Box (4 or U), or Equation (6 or E)
New Number (3 or N)

Renumbers all graphics boxes of a particular style beyond the
cursor position. You must rewrite the screen by using the

cursor movement keys or the Rewrite Screen feature for the
new numbering to take effect.

Options

GRAPHICS (ALT+F9) key
Figure (1 or F), Table Box (2 or T), Text Box (3 or B),
    User Box (4 or U), or Equation (6 or E)
Options (4 or O)

Alters any of the initial settings for how figures, table boxes,
text boxes, user-defined boxes, or equation boxes will appear
in a particular printed document, including the following:

- Border Style: Sets the style for the borders of the
  box.

- Border Space: Sets the amount of space between
  each box border and the text inside or outside the
  box.

- Numbering Method: Sets the numbering for the box.

- Caption: Determines the style for the caption and the
  caption position.

- Minimum Offset: Sets the limit for how much
  WordPerfect can reduce an offset measurement for a
  paragraph type.

- Shading: Determines the shading within the box.

▶ **GRAPHICS LINES**

Horizontal

> GRAPHICS (ALT+F9) key
> Line (5 or L)
> Create Line Horizontal (1 or H) or Edit Line Horizontal
>   (3 or O)

Inserts a horizontal line at the cursor or edits an existing line whose code is located above the cursor position. WordPerfect displays a menu on which you define the line's characteristics, including 1) the horizontal position where the line begins or extends to, 2) the vertical position for the line, 3) the length of the line across the page, 4) the thickness of the line, and 5) the percentage of shading, where 100% is black. The graphics line displays on the printed page but not on the Typing screen.

Vertical

> GRAPHICS (ALT+F9) key
> Line (5 or L)
> Create Line Vertical (2 or V) or Edit Line Vertical
>   (4 or E)

Inserts a vertical line at the cursor or edits an existing line whose code is located above the cursor position. WordPerfect displays a menu on which you define the line's characteristics, including 1) the horizontal position for the line, 2) the vertical position where the line begins or extends to, 3) the length of the line down the page, 4) the thickness of the line, and 5) the percentage of shading, where 100% is black. The graphics line displays on the printed page, but not on the Typing screen.

► GRAPHICS QUALITY

See TEXT/GRAPHICS QUALITY

► GRAPHICS SCREEN TYPE

See DISPLAY

► HANGING PARAGRAPH

See INDENT

► HARD PAGE

See PAGE BREAKS

► HARD RETURN

See RETURN

► HARD SPACE

HOME, SPACEBAR

Inserts a space which "glues" two words together so they will
not be split up by wordwrap. Useful for keeping the text of an
address or date on the same line.

► HEADERS/FOOTERS

Create

FORMAT (SHIFT+F8) key
Page (2 or P)
Headers (3 or H) or Footers (4 or F)
A (1 or A) or B (2 or B)
Every Page (2 or P), Odd Pages (3 or O), or Even Pages
    (4 or V)

Inserts standard lines of text at the top of pages (header) or at the bottom of pages (footer). The headers or footers appear on the printed page but not on the Typing screen.

Make sure to position the cursor at the top of the first page where you want the header or footer to print before following the key sequence. When the header or footer Typing screen appears, type in the text of the header or footer. Pressing CTRL+B within the text of the header or footer inserts the symbol ^B, which is replaced by a page number when the document is printed. (See SUPPRESS FOR CURRENT PAGE for the procedure to suppress headers and footers for a specific page in a document. Also see PAGE NUMBER-ING for the procedure to insert page numbers independent of headers and footers.)

Discontinue

FORMAT (SHIFT+F8) key
Page (2 or P)
Headers (3 or H) or Footers (4 or F)
A (1 or A) or B (2 or B)
Discontinue (1 or D)

Discontinues the header or footer specified to the end of the document (or until the next header or footer of that type is created further ahead in the text).

Edit

FORMAT (SHIFT+F8) key
Page (2 or P)
Headers (3 or H) or Footers (4 or F)
A (1 or A) or B (2 or B)
Edit (5 or E)

Edits a header or footer that you previously created and whose code is located above the cursor position.

► HELP

HELP (F3) key
Function key or letter (A-Z)

Provides on-line assistance with the functions and features of WordPerfect. Press SPACEBAR or ENTER to return to the document.

HELP is also context-sensitive, so if you press HELP while in a menu, a help screen describing the options for that menu will be displayed.

► HIGHLIGHT TEXT

See BLOCK

► HYPHEN TYPES

Character

HYPHEN

Inserts a hyphen that will remain between two words. The words may become split by wordwrap on separate lines if they fall at the end of a line.

Dash

HOME, HYPHEN, HYPHEN

Inserts a dash, which is a double hyphen, into the text. The two hyphens will remain together on the same line and will not be separated by wordwrap.

Hard

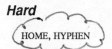

HOME, HYPHEN

Inserts a hyphen which "glues" two words together so that they will not be split up by wordwrap. Useful to serve as a minus sign in an equation or for keeping hyphenated phrases (such as mother-in-law) on the same line (see also HARD SPACE).

Soft

CTRL+HYPHEN

Inserts a hyphen that will appear only if a word falls at the end of a line in the Hyphenation Zone so that it requires hyphenation. This is useful if you wish to perform manual hyphenation. The hyphen disappears if you edit the text and the word no longer falls at the end of a line (see also HYPHENATION).

▶ HYPHENATION

Cancel for One Word

CANCEL (F1) key

When manual hyphenation is on and WordPerfect prompts for a hyphen location, CANCEL positions the whole word on the next line, without hyphenation.

Cancel for the Current Operation Only

EXIT (F7) key

When manual hyphenation is on and you begin an operation (such as a cursor movement command or the Spell feature) that results in WordPerfect prompting for a hyphen location, EXIT turns off hyphenation until the current operation is completed.

Turn On/Off

FORMAT (SHIFT+F8) key
Line (1 or L)
Hyphenation (1 or Y)
Y or N

Turns hyphenation on or off. You can turn on hyphenation before you type a document or after typing. Position the cursor at the top of the document (or where you want hyphenation to begin) before following the key sequence.

When hyphenation is off, words that do not fit within the Hyphenation Zone are wrapped down to the next line. When hyphenation is on, WordPerfect checks for hyphenation candidates that fall within the Hyphenation Zone as you type or move the cursor through existing text. WordPerfect hyphenates a word by inserting a soft hyphen. Depending on how you set up hyphenation to operate (see ENVIRONMENT), WordPerfect may prompt you for the hyphen location, as in this example:

Position hyphen; Press ESC configuration.

Move the hyphen with the left and right arrow keys and press ESC to insert a soft hyphen at the location you desire.

► HYPHENATION ZONE

FORMAT (SHIFT+F8) key
Line (1 or L)
Hyphenation Zone (2 or Z)

Determines the position boundaries within which word hyphenation will occur when hyphenation is on. The left and right Hyphenation Zone boundaries are expressed as a percentage of the line length from the right margin location. A word will be hyphenated if it starts at or before the left Hyphenation Zone and extends past the right Hyphenation Zone.

Enter left and right Hyphenation Zone settings as a percent of the line length. If you reduce the left or right Hyphenation

Zone percent settings, this narrows the Hyphenation Zone, so that more words will become hyphenation candidates. If you increase a percent setting, fewer words become hyphenation candidates.

► # INDENT

Left

⇒INDENT (F4) key

Indents the left side of a paragraph (text that ends with a hard return code). The paragraph is indented one tab stop each time you press ⇒INDENT.

This is useful for indenting a whole paragraph of text following a paragraph number or bullet and is also useful for creating a hanging paragraph, where all but the first line of text is indented. Create a hanging paragraph by pressing ⇒INDENT (F4), pressing SHIFT+TAB (which is the Left Margin Release), and then typing the paragraph.

Left/Right

⇒INDENT⇐ (SHIFT+F4) key

Indents both sides of a paragraph. The left side of the paragraph is indented one tab stop each time that you press ⇒INDENT⇐, and the right side is indented by an equal amount. Useful for indenting a long quote.

► INDEXES

Create Concordance File

Type the word or phrase to be included in an index and
press ENTER, so there is only one entry on each line.
Save the concordance file like a regular document.

Avoids the need to mark a phrase individually every time it
occurs in a document. When the index is generated, Word-
Perfect will search the document for all phrases contained in
the concordance file, just as if you marked each one yourself
and include the corresponding page numbers in the index.
Creating a concordance file does not exclude you from also
marking phrases individually in the text.

When WordPerfect generates the index, the concordance
file phrases are assumed to be headings. To denote certain
phrases as subheadings, mark those phrases in the concordance file just as you mark text in the document. (See *Mark
Text For*.)

Define

MARK TEXT (ALT+F5) key
Define (5 or D)
Define Index (3 or I)
Enter the concordance filename (or press ENTER if none)
Select a numbering style

Defines the location and page numbering style of the index
for when it is generated.

Generate

Generates an index after you have marked the entries for the index (and/or created a concordance file) and defined the index (see GENERATE CROSS-REFERENCES, END-NOTES, INDEXES, LISTS, TABLES for the key sequence).

Mark Text For

One word	MARK TEXT (ALT+F5) key
	Index (3 or I)
	Enter heading
	Enter subheading
Many words	Block the text
	MARK TEXT (ALT+F5) key
	Index (3 or I)
	Enter heading
	Enter subheading

Marks a word or phrase you wish to be included in the index when generated.

► INITIAL BASE FONT

See FONT

▶ INITIAL CODES

Document

FORMAT (SHIFT+F8) key
Document (3 or D)
Initial Codes (2 or C)

Controls the default format settings for the document currently on screen. Codes on the Document Initial Codes screen override the initial codes from the Setup menu (see *Setup*). Conversely, codes on the Document Initial Codes screen can be overridden by any format codes placed directly in the actual text of the document.

It is useful to insert format codes on the Document Initial Codes screen, rather than in the document itself, when you wish to activate a format change starting at the beginning of a document; it reduces the potential clutter of codes at the top of a document.

Setup

SETUP (SHIFT+F1) key
Initial Settings (4 or I)
Initial Codes (5 or C)

Controls the default format settings for every new document created. Format codes that you insert on the Setup Initial Codes screen override the initial format settings as set up by WordPerfect. The initial format settings as set up by WordPerfect include the following:

Margins	1"
(top/bottom/left/right)	
Justification	Full
Hyphenation	Off
Tabs	Every 0 .5"
Line Spacing	Single spacing
Page Size/Type	8.5" x 11"/standard
Page Numbering	None
Widow/Orphan	Off

However, codes inserted on the Setup Initial Codes screen can be overridden by any format codes placed on the Document Initial Codes screen (see *Document*) or directly in the actual text of the document.

It is useful to insert format codes on the Setup Initial Codes screen when you wish to activate a format change for the majority of documents that you will create from now on.

► INITIAL SETTINGS

SETUP (SHIFT+F1) key
Initial Settings (4 or I)

Alters settings for how certain features should initially operate, including Date Format, Equations, Print Options, Repeat Value, Merge Delimiters, and Table of Authorities (see these separate entries). Also, this menu alters how all new documents should be initially formatted (see INITIAL CODES). In addition, you can specify whether all retrieved documents are formatted for the default (currently selected) printer or are instead formatted for the printer that was selected when the document was last saved to disk.

▶ INITIALIZE PRINTER

See DOWNLOADABLE (SOFT) FONTS

▶ INTERNATIONAL CHARACTERS

See COMPOSE

▶ ITALICS

Prints text in italics (slanted to the right), based on the base font (see APPEARANCE for the key sequence).

▶ INSERT MODE

INS (only necessary if currently in Typeover mode)

Characters you type are inserted at the cursor, and existing characters are pushed to the right to make room for the new characters. The INS key is a toggle that switches between Insert and Typeover modes. (See also TYPEOVER MODE.)

▶ JUSTIFICATION

FORMAT (SHIFT+F8) key
Line (1 or L)
Justification (3 or J)
Left (1 or L), Center (2 or C), Right (3 or R), or
    Full (4 or F)

Determines how text is aligned in relation to the left and right margins. Left justification results in an even left margin and a ragged right margin; right justification has the opposite outcome. Center justification positions each line equidistant from the left and right margins. Full justification results in extra spaces being inserted on each line in paragraphs to make both the left and right margin even when the text is printed. Full justification appears on the printed page, but appears on the Typing screen with a ragged right margin, as if left justification were in effect.

▶ KEEP TEXT TOGETHER

See PROTECT, BLOCK, CONDITIONAL END OF PAGE, and WIDOW/ORPHAN PROTECTION

▶ KERNING

FORMAT (SHIFT+F8) key
Other (4 or O)
Printer Functions (6 or P)
Kerning (1 or K)
Y or N

Allows for the reduction of space between certain letter pairs, such as WA or VO. The kerning is based on the kerning tables for the printer that is used to print out your document. (Not all printers have defined kerning tables, so kerning may have no effect on your document.)

▶ KEYBOARD LAYOUT

Create

SETUP (SHIFT+F1) key
Keyboard Layout (5 or K)
Create (4 or C)

Establishes a keyboard definition, where a keyboard definition alters the function assigned by WordPerfect Corporation to one or more keys on the keyboard. Within a keyboard definition, keys such as [, ALT+1, CTRL+S, or SHIFT+F2 can be defined to 1) activate a certain command, 2) insert a special character, or 3) execute a macro. Once you create a keyboard definition, it will only become active when you select it (see *Turn On*). This is useful for tailoring the keyboard to your own personal needs.

When WordPerfect prompts "Keyboard Filename:", enter a filename for the keyboard definition you are about to create; WordPerfect automatically assigns the extension .WPK to that filename. Next, select Edit (7 or E); the Keyboard Edit screen appears, on which you can 1) select Create (4 or C) to create an assignment for a certain key, 2) position the cursor on a key and select Action (1 or A) to alter an existing key assignment, 3) position the cursor on a key and select Description (2 or D) to create or edit an explanation of that key's assignment, or 4) manage a key assignment by positioning the cursor and selecting Move (5 or M) or Original (3 or O), which returns the key to its original assignment. You can also work with macros and key definitions: select Save (6 or S) to save a key assignment as a macro, or select Retrieve (7 or R) to assign an already created macro to a key.

Drive/Directory Location

Determines where on disk keyboard definition files (with the file extension .WPK) are stored (see LOCATION OF FILES).

Manage

> SETUP (SHIFT+F1) key
> Keyboard Layout (5 or K)
> Delete (2 or D), Rename (3 or R), Copy (5 or Y), Edit
>   (7 or E), Map (8 or M), or Name Search (N)

Allows you to manipulate existing key definitions. You can delete, rename, or copy a definition by positioning the cursor on a keyboard definition name and selecting the corresponding menu item. Or, edit a keyboard definition by positioning the cursor and selecting Edit (7 or E). You can view a map of all the keys that have been reassigned (except for function and cursor movement keys) by positioning the cursor and selecting Map (8 or M). The Map menu item also enables you to alter key assignments. If you select the Name Search menu item, you can position the cursor on a keyboard definition without using the arrow keys; instead, type the beginning letters of the key definition name until the cursor moves there. Press ENTER to end Name Search.

Turn On

> SETUP (SHIFT+F1) key
> Keyboard Layout (5 or K)
> Position cursor on keyboard definition name
> Select (1 or S)

Turns on (selects) a specific keyboard definition. Once a keyboard definition is selected, all keys abide by their assigned function.

Turn Off

> SETUP (SHIFT+F1) key
> Keyboard Layout (5 or K)
> Original (6 or O)

Turns off the active keyboard definition, returning the keyboard to its original functions as set up by WordPerfect Corporation. (An alternative to the key sequence just shown is simply to press CTRL+6, which turns off the active keyboard definition for the rest of the working session.)

► LABELS

See ENVELOPES AND LABELS

► LANGUAGE

> FORMAT (SHIFT+F8) key
> Other (4 or O)
> Language (4 or L)
> Enter a language code

Indicates to WordPerfect the language of the current document and that you wish to use a foreign language speller, thesaurus, and/or hyphenation file that is on disk. The current language also determines the language used for the Date and

Sort features. The language codes used in WordPerfect include:

AF	Afrikaans	IT	Italian
BR	Portuguese, Brazil	NL	Dutch
CF	French, Canadian	NO	Norwegian
CA	Catalonian	OZ	English, Australian
CZ	Czechoslovakian	PO	Portuguese, Portugal
DK	Danish	RU	Russian
DE	German	SD	German, Swiss
ES	Spanish	SU	Finnish
FR	French	SV	Swedish
GR	Greek	US	English, United States
IS	Icelandic	UK	English, United Kingdom

► LARGE

Prints text in large (next dimension up from normal) size characters for the base font (see SIZE for the key sequence).

► LEADING

FORMAT (SHIFT+F8) key
Other (4 or O)
Printer Functions (6 or P)
Leading Adjustment (6 or L)

Dictates the amount of extra space between lines of text, which is in addition to the 2 points of leading automatically added for proportionally spaced fonts. (Leading for monospaced fonts is built in.)

Enter a leading measurement both for lines that end with soft return codes, which are those within paragraphs, and for lines that end with hard return codes, which are those that separate paragraphs.

► LEFT MARGIN RELEASE

See MARGIN RELEASE

► LINE DRAW

SCREEN (CTRL+F3) key
Line Draw (2 or L)

Draws boxes, graphs, and other pictures on screen when you use the arrow keys. This feature operates in Typeover mode and does not work properly with a proportionally spaced font.

From the Line Draw menu, you can select to draw with various draw characters, including a single line (option 1), a double line (option 2), an asterisk (option 3), or various shaded boxes of different heights and widths (option 4). You also can erase lines you have drawn (option 5) or move the cursor without drawing (option 6).

► LINE FORMAT

See FORMAT

▶ LINE HEIGHT

FORMAT (SHIFT+F8) key
Line (1 or L)
Line Height (4 or H)
Auto (1 or A) or Fixed (2 or F)

Sets the amount of vertical space allotted for each line when printed. The line height is determined by WordPerfect based on the printer that will be used to print your document. When set to Auto, the assumed line height is used but will be adjusted whenever a font or font attribute change alters the size of the characters to be printed. When set to Fixed, line height remains evenly spaced regardless of the font or font attribute you are using. (See also LEADING to add additional space between lines.)

For the Auto menu item, WordPerfect automatically sets the line height to the printer's assumed setting. For the Fixed menu item, WordPerfect displays the assumed line height setting; press ENTER to accept that suggestion, or enter a different line height setting.

▶ LINE NUMBERING

FORMAT (SHIFT+F8) key
Line (1 or L)
Line Numbering (5 or N)
Y or N

Turns line numbering on or off. With line numbering on, line numbers are inserted near the left margin when the document is printed. Line numbering does not appear on the Typing screen. It is useful in legal documents or for reference purposes when calling attention to specific line numbers in a document.

Type **Y** to turn line numbering on or **N** to turn it off. When line numbering is turned on, a Line Numbering screen appears, enabling you to define how the numbering should occur: whether to count blank lines in the numbering (option 1), the frequency with which lines are numbered (option 2), the position for the line numbers (option 3), the starting line number (option 4), and whether to restart numbering on each page (option 5).

► LINE SPACING

FORMAT (SHIFT+F8) key
Line (1 or L)
Line Spacing (6 or S)

Alters the spacing between lines of text. The line spacing number is multiplied by the line height to determine the new line spacing. (See also LINE HEIGHT.) WordPerfect displays on screen the line spacing in whole-number increments only.

Enter a new line spacing number, such as 1/2 or 0.5 for half spacing, 1 for single spacing, 1.5 for one-and-one-half spacing, 2 for double spacing, and so on. Some printers can even support fractional line spacing, such as 1.3 line spacing.

► LIST FILES

LIST (F5) key
Type in drive or directory name and press ENTER

Offers information about the files in the indicated drive or directory. The header at the top of the List Files screen also provides the information about the current date and time, the drive or directory for which files are now displayed, the size of the document currently on the Typing screen (in bytes), the free disk space (also in bytes) still available for storing files, the amount of space occupied on that drive or directory, and the number of files in the current drive or directory.

The middle of the List Files screen displays the names of files on the drive or directory indicated, along with each file's size (measured in bytes, where a byte equals approximately one character) and the date and time that file was last saved to disk.

A menu at the bottom of the List Files screen enables you to manage files on disk. (See also COPY FILES, DEFAULT DRIVE/DIRECTORY, DELETE FILES, FIND FILES, MOVE/RENAME FILES, PRINT, RETRIEVE A FILE, SHORT/LONG DISPLAY, LOOK, and NAME SEARCH.)

To print the List Files screen that you are viewing, press PRINT (SHIFT+F7).

► LISTS

Define

MARK TEXT (ALT+F5) key
Define (5 or D)
Define List (2 or L)
Enter a list number
Select a numbering style

Defines the location and page numbering style of the list for when it is generated. You can define up to ten lists in each document.

Generate

Generates a list after you have marked the text for the list and defined the list. You may create lists for illustrations, charts, or graphics boxes (whether for a figure, table, text box, or user-defined box; see GRAPHICS BOXES). Up to ten lists can be generated, one for each list definition mark inserted in the document. (See GENERATE CROSS-REFERENCES, ENDNOTES, INDEXES, LISTS, TABLES for the key sequence.)

Mark Text For

Block the text
MARK TEXT (ALT+F5) key
List (2 or L)
Enter list number

Marks a word or phrase you wish to be included in a list when generated.

► LOCATION OF FILES

SETUP (SHIFT+F1) key
Location of Files (6 or L)

Indicates to WordPerfect where certain auxiliary files are housed. Useful if you wish to organize your files on disk such that these other files are stored in a drive or directory other than where the main WordPerfect program file WP.EXE is housed (or other than the current default drive or directory in the case of the backup, macro, and keyboard definition files). The options for auxiliary files include the following:

- Backup directory: Specifies the drive or directory where the timed backup files WP{WP}.BK1 and WP{WP}.BK2 will be stored (see also BACKUP).

- Keyboard/macro files: Specifies the drive or directory where all keyboard definitions (which end with the extension .WPK) and all macros (which end with the extension .WPM) are stored (see also MACROS and KEYBOARD LAYOUT).

- Main dictionary: Specifies the drive or directory where the main dictionary, thesaurus, and hyphenation files are stored. (As an example, the U.S. version of the main dictionary is named WP{WP}US.LEX, the thesaurus is WP{WP}-US.THS and the hyphenation module is WP{WP}US.HYC.)

- Supplementary dictionary: Specifies the drive or directory where the words that you add to the dictionary in a supplementary file are stored. (As an example, the U.S. version of the supplemental dictionary is named WP{WP}US.SUP.)

- Printer files: Specifies the drive or directory where the files that contain the printer drivers (files with the extension .ALL or .PRS) are stored (see also PRINTER, SELECT).

- Style files and library file: Specifies the drive or directory where the styles files are stored and designates a certain file that will serve as the style library, so when you create a new document and press the STYLE (ALT+F8) key, the styles in that file are automatically displayed. For the style library filename, you must indicate not only a drive or directory, but also a filename. (See also STYLES.)

- Graphic files: Specifies the drive or directory where files containing graphics images (such as files with the extension .WPG) are stored.

- Documents: Specifies the default drive or directory for documents that WordPerfect will assume at the start of every working session. The default is the location files are retrieved from or stored to. (See also DEFAULT DRIVE/DIRECTORY, CHANGE for the procedure to change the default in a workir.￼ session.)

► LOCK/UNLOCK FILES

Lock

TEXT IN/OUT (CTRL+F5) key
Password (2 or P)
Add/Change (1 or A)
Enter a password twice

Locks a file so that its contents cannot be retrieved, looked at, or printed without use of the proper password. Useful for ensuring that a document on disk remains confidential. You must remember the password or you will be locked out of the file.

Enter a password that contains 24 characters or less. When you enter the password, it does not appear on screen; thus, you enter it twice to make sure you are not making a typing mistake. After adding (or changing) the password, remember to resave the file so that the password is attached to the document permanently (or until you unlock the file).

Unlock

TEXT IN/OUT (CTRL+F5) key
Password (2 or P)
Remove (2 or R)

Unlocks a previously locked document. After unlocking the file, remember to resave the file so that the password is removed from the document permanently (or until you add a password again).

► LONG DOCUMENT NAMES

SETUP (SHIFT+F1) key
Environment (3 or E)
Document Management/Summary (4 or D)
Long Document Names (3 or L)
Y or N

Enables you to assign descriptive document names to your files, rather than being restricted to the standard, short (8-character) filename. A long document name can be up to 68 characters in length, contain a filename extension of up to 20 characters, and contain spaces. At the same time, a document type can also be assigned to further describe each file.

If the Long Document Name feature is activated, Word-Perfect will prompt you for the long document name and the document type before prompting you for the short (8-character) name whenever you save a file. In addition, the List Files screen will be set automatically to the long document display at the start of each working session so the long document names are shown (see SHORT/LONG DISPLAY). If you establish a default document type, that type is always suggested whenever WordPerfect prompts for a document type (see DEFAULT DOCUMENT TYPE.) The long document name is referred to as the "Document Name" in a summary (see SUMMARY).

LOOK

LIST (F5) key
Type drive or directory name and press ENTER
Position cursor on a filename
Look (6 or L) or ENTER

Shows the contents of a file on disk without disrupting the document currently on the Typing screen. The text is displayed, but not the WordPerfect format of that file.

If a document summary exists for the file (see SUMMARY), the summary is displayed first; select from the menu items at the bottom of the screen or press the down arrow key to see the text of the file. Use the cursor movement keys to move up and down through the text of the file. Use the Search feature to move the cursor to a specific section of text (see SEARCH), or select from the other menu items at the bottom of the screen to look at the contents of the next or previous document. You cannot edit a document in the Look screen.

MACROS

Define

MACRO DEFINE (CTRL+F10) key
Enter macro name
Enter macro description
Type sequence of keystrokes
MACRO DEFINE (CTRL+F10) key

Records a macro, where a macro is a sequence of keystrokes that WordPerfect memorizes and can be executed at your command. Name a macro with from one to eight letters or with the ALT key plus a letter; WordPerfect adds the extension .WPM to the filename when stored on disk. You can name the default macro by pressing only the ENTER key, in which case you are not prompted for a macro description and the macro is stored with the name WP{WP}.WPM.

When WordPerfect prompts "Define macro:", enter a macro name. When WordPerfect prompts "Description:", type in a description up to 39 characters in length.

Drive/Directory Location

Determines where on disk macro files (with the file extension .WPM) are stored (see LOCATION OF FILES).

Edit Description

MACRO DEFINE (CTRL+F10) key
Enter previously created macro name
Description (3 or D)

Edits the macro description that is created when a macro is first defined. The macro description is displayed when you edit a macro on the Macro Action screen or when you use the Look feature on the List Files screen to view the contents of a macro file.

Edit Keystrokes (or Add Programming Commands)

MACRO DEFINE (CTRL+F10) key
Enter previously created macro name
Edit (2 or E)

Adds or deletes keystrokes that comprise a macro and provides access to the Macro Programming Language. (You can edit all macros except the default macro, which is named with the ENTER key.)

On the Macro Action screen, use the standard typing and editing keys to delete or insert keystrokes. To insert editing keystrokes such as {Backspace} or {Exit} as part of the macro, either 1) press MACRO DEFINE (CTRL+F10), type as many editing keystrokes as necessary, and press MACRO DEFINE again, or 2) press CTRL+V before pressing an editing key.

While on the Macro Action screen, you have access to the Macro Programming Language. With this language, all the sophistication of programming is possible for macros. Press CTRL+PGUP to display a list of programming language commands. To insert a command, move the cursor on that command and press EXIT (F7) or ENTER; the command is inserted in the macro wherever your cursor was located before you pressed CTRL+PGUP. To leave the Macro Programming Language commands without inserting a command, press CANCEL (F1) or ESC.

Execute

Named with ALT key	ALT + letter key
Not named with ALT key	MACRO (ALT+F10) key Type macro name and press ENTER

Invokes a macro. You can also assign a macro to a key as part of a keyboard definition. In that case, you can execute the macro once the keyboard definition has been selected by pressing the corresponding key (see KEYBOARD LAYOUT).

Options

CTRL+PGUP
Pause (1 or P), Display (2 or D), Assign (3 or A), or
    Comment (4 or C)

Inserts a special macro command within a macro. Press CTRL+PGUP while defining a macro wherever you wish the special macro option to take effect. The four options are

- Pause: During macro execution, brings a macro to a temporary stop so that different text or commands can be typed in each time a macro is executed. While defining the macro, make sure to type in a sample of the text or commands to be inserted during the pause, and press ENTER. During macro execution, press ENTER after typing in the text or commands at the pause.

- Display: Either turns display on or off for the macro execution. Off is the default, meaning that unless you turn it on, the macro execution is invisible.

- Assign: Passes a value to a variable, which is useful for when you are creating a sophisticated macro using the Macro Programming Language. When WordPerfect prompts "Variable:", type a number from 0 to 9. When WordPerfect prompts "Value:", type in the value that you wish to assign.

- Comment: Inserts a comment into the macro so that the keystrokes are easy to read and decipher on the Macro Action screen. A comment has no effect on macro execution. (You can also insert a comment with the Macro Programming Language.)

Replace

MACRO DEFINE (CTRL+F10) key
Enter previously created macro name
Replace (1 or R)

Overwrites the existing macro with a new macro that you define.

► MAIL MERGE

See MERGE

► MAILING LABELS

See ENVELOPES AND LABELS

▶ ⇐MARGIN RELEASE

SHIFT+TAB key

Moves the cursor back to the previous tab stop. If the cursor is at the left margin when SHIFT+TAB is pressed, the cursor moves to the tab stop left of the left margin.

Press ⇒INDENT and then SHIFT+TAB to create a hanging paragraph, where the first line of the paragraph begins one tab stop to the left of the rest of the paragraph lines (see also INDENT).

▶ MARGINS

Left/Right

FORMAT (SHIFT+F8) key
Line (1 or L)
Margins Left/Right (7 or M)

Changes the left and/or right margins for the document or a portion of that document when printed. Enter both a left and right margin setting (in inches, centimeters, points, or version 4.2 horizontal units).

Top/Bottom

FORMAT (SHIFT+F8) key
Page (2 or P)
Margins Top/Bottom (5 or M)

Changes the top and/or bottom margins for the document or portion of that document when printed. Enter both a top and bottom margin setting (in inches, centimeters, points, or version 4.2 vertical units).

▶ MARK FILES

LIST (F5) key
Type drive or directory name and press ENTER
Position cursor on a filename
Type asterisk (*)

Marks specific files with an asterisk on the List Files screen, so that an operation such as deleting, printing, moving, copying, or using the Find feature can be performed on many files at once.

The asterisk acts like a toggle switch; press it once to mark the highlighted file or press it twice to unmark the file. You can mark all files on the List Files screen if none are marked by pressing MARK TEXT (ALT+F5) or HOME, *. If some files are marked, press MARK TEXT (ALT+F5) or HOME, * to unmark all files.

After specific files are marked and you select an option on the List Files menu, a WordPerfect prompt asks whether it is the marked files on which you wish to perform the command. Type **Y** to perform the command on all the marked files, or type **N** to perform the command on the highlighted file only.

▶ MARK TEXT

Marks text for use with special WordPerfect features (see
CROSS-REFERENCE, MASTER DOCUMENTS, IN-
DEXES, TABLES OF AUTHORITIES, TABLES OF CON-
TENTS, and LISTS).

▶ MASTER DOCUMENTS

Create

> Position cursor in master where subdocument is to be
>   located
> MARK TEXT (ALT+F5) key
> Subdocument (2 or S)

Allows for efficient editing and management of long documents. Separate parts of a long document are stored in individual files, called subdocuments, and are linked together in
proper order via the master document. This is useful for books
that contain numerous chapters or for reports that contain
many sections.

When WordPerfect prompts "Subdoc filename:", enter the
filename of the text to be included at that location (preceded
by a specific drive or directory if different from the default).
WordPerfect marks the subdocument location on screen by
displaying a comment in a single-line box that reads "Subdoc:" and lists the subdocument filename.

To print the complete document, including the master and
all subdocuments, expand the master document (see *Ex-
pand/Condense*).

Expand/Condense

Master document must be on screen
MARK TEXT (ALT+F5) key
Generate (6 or G)
Expand (3 or E) or Condense (4 or O)

Expands a master document so you can review and edit the text of the master and all subdocuments at once or print the text in its entirety. Condense a master document into its original short form before saving the master again to disk.

Before expanding a master document, make sure that all subdocuments have been typed and stored on disk. If, when expanding, WordPerfect cannot locate the name of a subdocument listed in the master, it prompts with a "Subdoc not found" message. Press ENTER to skip that subdocument and continue the expansion, or press CANCEL (F1) to abort the expansion. Once expanded, the document's numbering and option codes for features such as cross-references, footnotes, endnotes, and page numbers remain consecutively numbered and consistent throughout the text.

When condensing a master document, WordPerfect prompts "Save Subdocs?". Type **Y** if you have made editing changes to any of the subdocuments, in which case the WordPerfect program will request a decision on saving each of the subdocuments. Type **N** if you made no editing changes to the text of the subdocuments.

MATH COLUMNS

Calculate

COLUMNS/TABLES (ALT+F7) key
Math (3 or M)
Calculate (4 or A)

Calculates the results for any math operators placed in the math columns. You can only calculate in that portion of a document where Math has been turned on.

Calculate your math columns as a last step after defining your columns (if necessary), turning Math on, typing in numbers and math operators so that they are aligned on tab stops, and turning Math off.

Position the cursor between the Math On and Math Off codes before beginning this key sequence.

See TABLES for the procedure to calculate within tables.

Define

COLUMNS/TABLES (ALT+F7) key
Math (3 or M)
Define (3 or D)

Defines your math column layout, the first basic step to creating columns if you wish to calculate down columns while changing the default math column settings or to calculate across columns. (Defining columns is generally unnecessary if you wish to perform simple addition down columns.) You may wish to change tab stop locations before defining your column layout.

On the Math Definition screen that displays, you define from 2 to 24 columns, specifying 1) the type of columns (numeric, total, text, or calculation), 2) how negative numbers are displayed, 3) the number of digits to the right of the decimal in calculated results, and 4) the formulas for calculation columns. You can only define columns where Math is turned off.

For a calculation column, you must define a math formula on the Math Definition screen, using the following symbols when writing the formula:

+	Addition
-	Subtraction
*	Multiplication
/	Division

You also can insert the following special formulas on their own:

+	Add all numeric columns
+/	Average of all numeric columns
=	Add all total columns
=/	Average of all total columns

Operators

Press TAB until at correct tab stop
Type in a math operator

Inserts a math operator at the location where you want a calculation to occur. Type math operators only after Math has been turned on. A math operator must be aligned on a tab stop to operate properly.

The math operator you insert depends on the calculation you desire:

+   Subtotal
=   Total
*   Grand total

Or, type **t** in front of a known subtotal, **T** in front of a known total, or **N** in front of a calculated total that you want treated as negative.

If a math column has been defined as a calculation column, when you press TAB to move to that column, WordPerfect inserts the math operator ! on its own, signifying that the result will display in that location after the math columns are calculated.

Turn On/Off

COLUMNS/TABLES (ALT+F7) key
Math (3 or M)
On (1 or O) or Off (2 or F)

Turns on or off the Math feature. Turn on Math after defining math columns (if you found it necessary to define math columns) but before typing numbers and math operators into the math columns. Turn off Math after typing all numbers and math operators into the math columns. The Math On and Math Off codes that are inserted mark the start and end of the math portion of the document like bookends.

▶ MENU OPTIONS

See DISPLAY

▶  MERGE

Convert Old Merge Codes

MERGE/SORT (CTRL+F9) key
Convert Old Merge Codes (3 or C)

Converts merge codes contained in the document on screen
from version 5.0 format (such as ^E or ^R) into version 5.1
format (such as {END RECORD} or {END FIELD}). Conversion is an option, but not a necessity, in order for version
5.0 merge files to operate properly in version 5.1.

End Field

END FIELD (F9) key

Inserts an {END FIELD} code followed by a hard return. This
merge code is inserted throughout a secondary merge file to
signify the end of each field.

Execute

MERGE/SORT (CTRL+F9) key
Merge (1 or M)
Enter primary document filename
Enter secondary document filename

This initiates a merge process. You can merge with a file or the keyboard.

When you merge with a file, the primary file contains the text that stays the same for each personalized document as well as {FIELD} and other merge codes that occupy the space where variable information will be inserted during the merge. The secondary file contains the variable information that personalizes each document. After the merge is complete, the cursor is at the bottom of the last merged document. Move the cursor to the top of the file that is on the screen to review starting with the first merged document.

When you merge with the keyboard, the primary file contains the text that stays the same for each personalized document as well as {INPUT} and other codes that occupy the space where you will insert variable information from the keyboard. There is no secondary file, so if you are merging with the keyboard, press ENTER without specifying a secondary filename. Unless you specify otherwise, only one document is merged each time you execute a merge with the keyboard.

File Delimiters

SETUP (SHIFT+F1) key
Initial Settings (4 or I)
Merge (1 or M)

Specifies how fields and records are separated in a DOS text file that will be used as your secondary merge file during a merge. To insert the DOS carriage return command [CR], press CTRL+M, and to insert the DOS line feed command [LF], press ENTER.

Insert Merge Codes

MERGE CODES (SHIFT+F9) key
Field (1 or F), End Record (2 or E), Input (3 or I), Page
    Off (4 or P), Next Record (5 or N), or More (6 or M)

Inserts a merge code into the text in order to create a primary
or secondary merge document. ({END FIELD} is the only
merge code that is not inserted into the text using the key
sequence just shown; see *End Field*). Merge codes include

{FIELD}*n~*	During a merge with a file, inserts the variable information contained in field number *n* of the secondary merge file into the location wherever the {FIELD} code is located in the primary file.
{END RECORD}	Marks the end of a record in a secondary merge file, and is followed by a hard page code.
{INPUT}*message~*	Indicates the location for a pause for input from the keyboard during a merge with the keyboard. The message is displayed on screen during the pause.
{PAGE OFF}	Inhibits WordPerfect from placing hard page codes in the text after each record in the secondary file is merged with the primary file.

{NEXT RECORD}   Causes the merge to continue
                  with the next record in the
                  secondary file.

Advanced merge code commands are also available for enhancing the merge process. To insert one of these commands, select the More option to display a list of the commands, move the cursor on the command that you wish to select, and press ENTER. Many of the advanced merge code commands are also part of the Macro Programming Language (see MACROS).

▶ MOUSE

For Activating Features

See the General Reminders section

For Marking a Block

Position mouse pointer at one end of the text
Press left mouse button and drag mouse pointer to
    opposite end of the text
Release left mouse button

Marks off (highlights) a portion of a document on which various commands can be performed. The message "Block on" flashes on the screen. (See also BLOCK.)

For Moving the Cursor

See the General Reminders section

Setup

SETUP (SHIFT+F1) key
Mouse (1 or M)

Defines the mouse type connected to your computer and how
the mouse will operate in WordPerfect, including

- Mouse type and port: The type of mouse (both the
  brand of mouse and whether it is serial or bus type)
  attached to your computer and the port (plug) at the
  back of the computer to which it is attached.

- Double-click interval: The interval for
  double-clicking, measured in 100ths of a second. If
  two clicks are not pressed within the specified
  interval, WordPerfect considers the movement as
  two single clicks rather than as a double-click.

- Submenu delay time: The time that the cursor must
  rest on a pull-down menu before its submenu
  displays, measured in 100ths of a second.

- Acceleration factor: The responsiveness of the
  mouse pointer on screen to movements of the
  mouse, where a greater acceleration factor means a
  more responsive mouse pointer.

- Left-handed mouse: Whether you will use the mouse
  with your left hand, so that the tasks performed by
  the right mouse button can be switched to the left
  mouse button and vice versa.

- Assisted mouse-pointer movement: Whether
  WordPerfect should move the mouse pointer

automatically to a line menu when the menu is displayed.

▶ MOVE/COPY

Block, Tabular Column, Rectangle

Block the text
MOVE (CTRL+F4) key
Block (1 or B), Tabular Column (2 or C), or Rectangle
   (3 or R)
Move (1 or M) or Copy (2 or C)
Reposition cursor
ENTER

Moves a highlighted block by cutting it from one location and inserting it in another; copies a block by leaving the block at one location and also inserting it in another.

The block can highlight not only a standard cluster of text, but a tabular column or rectangle. To highlight a tabular column, which is text or numbers aligned on a tab stop, position the cursor on any character in the first line of the column, press BLOCK (ALT+F4), and then position the cursor on any character in the last line of the column. When you press the Tabular Column menu item, only that one column will be highlighted. To highlight a rectangle, position the cursor on the character that represents the upper-left corner of the rectangle, press BLOCK (ALT+F4), and then use the cursor to highlight up to the character that represents the lower-right corner of the rectangle. When you press the Rectangle menu item, only the text that comprises that rectangle will be highlighted.

Retrieve Moved or Copied Text

MOVE (CTRL+F4) key
Retrieve (4 or R)
Block (1 or B), Tabular Column (2 or C), or Rectangle
   (3 or R)

Retrieves the most recently moved or copied block, tabular
column, or rectangle into the text at the current cursor position. This is useful for inserting the same text more than one
time into a document.

It is also useful when you want to move or copy text but
wish to wait until later on in the editing session to place that
text in a new location. When you follow the key sequence to
move or copy text and the message "Move cursor; press ENTER
to retrieve" appears after you have indicated the text to move
or copy, press CANCEL (F1); the message disappears. To
retrieve that text later on, follow the key sequence to retrieve
the text.

Sentence, Paragraph, Page

Position cursor within the sentence, paragraph, or page
MOVE (CTRL+F4) key
Sentence (1 or S), Paragraph (2 or P), or Page (3 or A)
Move (1 or M) or Copy (2 or C)
Reposition cursor
ENTER

Moves or copies 1) the current sentence that ends with a punctuation mark (period, question mark, or exclamation point) and is followed by a space, 2) the current paragraph that ends with a hard return code, or 3) the current page that ends with a soft or hard page break code.

► MOVE/RENAME FILES

LIST (F5) key
Type drive or directory name and press ENTER
Position cursor on a file
Move/Rename (3 or M)

Moves a selected file to another location or changes a filename. Useful if you desire to move a file to a more appropriate directory or provide a document with a more descriptive filename.

When WordPerfect prompts "New name:" with the drive or directory and name of the file, edit the prompt. If you change the drive or directory designation, the file is moved for you. If you change the filename, the file is renamed.

You can move two or more files in one command by marking the files you wish to move with an asterisk before selecting Move/Rename (see MARK FILES).

► MULTIPLE COPIES

PRINT (SHIFT+F7) key
Multiple Copies Generated by (U)

A print option that specifies who controls the number of copies of your text that are printed: WordPerfect or your printer. If your printer has the capability, the printing of multiple copies will be faster. The Multiple Copies feature is altered for every print job that you send to the printer from that point on until you again change it or until you exit WordPerfect.

▶ NAME SEARCH

LIST (F5) key
Type drive or directory name and press ENTER
Type N
Type first letters of filename
ENTER

On the List Files screen, moves the cursor to the filename that begins with the letters typed. This is a quick method for moving to a filename without using the arrow keys. (The Name Search feature is also found on other screens, such as the Style, Base Font, Initial Base Font, and Select Printer screens.)

▶ NEW PAGE

See PAGE BREAKS

► NEW PAGE NUMBER

FORMAT (SHIFT+F8) key
Page (2 or P)
Page Numbering (6 or N)
New Page Number (1 or N)

Renumbers all pages starting on the page where your cursor was located before you typed the key sequence. Make sure that the cursor is at the top of a page before initiating this feature.

When entering a new page number, you can specify Arabic style (1,2,3 and so on), uppercase Roman numerals (I, II, III, and so on) or lowercase Roman numerals (i, ii, iii and so on) by typing the number either as an Arabic number or a Roman numeral. The status line reflects the new page number, although Roman numerals are shown on the printed page and not on the status line.

► NUMBER OF COPIES

PRINT (SHIFT+F7) key
Number of Copies (N)

A print option that can specify the number of copies. This option is useful for producing multiple copies of documents in one print job. The number of copies is changed for every print job that you send to the printer from that point on until you again change it or until you exit WordPerfect.

▶ NUMBER LINES

See LINE NUMBERING

▶ NUMBER PAGES

See PAGE NUMBERING

▶ NUMBER PARAGRAPHS

See PARAGRAPH NUMBERING

▶ ORPHAN PROTECTION

See WIDOW/ORPHAN PROTECTION

▶ OTHER FORMAT

See FORMAT

▶ OUTLINE

Prints text where characters are in outline form (such as white letters silhouetted in blank ink), based on the base font (see APPEARANCE for the key sequence).

▶ OUTLINE STYLES

See STYLES

▶ OUTLINING

Define Numbering Style and Starting Number

DATE/OUTLINE (SHIFT+F5) key
Define (6 or D)
Paragraph (2 or P), Outline (3 or O), Legal (4 or L),
    Bullets (5 or B), User-Defined (6 or U), or Outline
    Style Name (9 or N) to select a style
Starting Paragraph Number (1 or S)
Type a starting number

Specifies the numbering style for the outline numbers, where the default is Outline Numbering style with the following eight levels:

I., A., 1., a., (1), (a), i), a)

You can select from predefined styles (Paragraph, Outline, Legal, or Bullets) or select the User-Defined menu item, in which case you must indicate the numbering style for each level. Or, you can instead specify an outline style name and turn on that style (see STYLES).

You can also specify what number the outline will begin with, which is most useful when you wish to create two outlines in the same document or when you wish to continue numbering between different files. To begin numbering at 1, the default setting, there is no need to select the Starting Paragraph Number menu item.

Define Outlining Procedure for ENTER key

DATE/OUTLINE (SHIFT+F5) key
Define (6 or D)
Enter Inserts Paragraph Number (7 or E) or
    Automatically Adjust to Current Level (8 or A)

Determines whether pressing the ENTER key when Outline is on inserts an outline (paragraph) number. If you set this option to No, then use the Paragraph Numbering feature to insert outline numbers (see PARAGRAPH NUMBERING). Also determines whether, when you press ENTER to insert an outline number, WordPerfect inserts a new outline number at the current level, which is the level of the most recent outline number inserted, or instead returns the cursor to the left margin and inserts an outline number at level 1.

Move/Copy/Delete Family

DATE/OUTLINE (SHIFT+F5) key
Outline (4 or O)
Move Family (3 or M), Copy Family (4 or C), or Delete
    Family (5 or D)

Moves, copies, or deletes an entire outline family, where an outline family is the outline level on the line where the cursor is located plus any lower levels. Make sure that Outline is on and that the cursor is positioned on the first line of the family that you wish to move, copy, or delete before following the key sequence just shown.

WordPerfect highlights the outline family in reverse video. For moving, use the arrow keys to reposition the outline family, and press ENTER. For copying, use the arrow keys to reposition the copy of the outline family that is created, and press ENTER. For deleting, type **Y** to verify the deletion of the outline family.

Turn On/Off

DATE/OUTLINE (SHIFT+F5) key
Outline (4 or O)
On (1 or O) or Off (2 or F)

Turns on Outline when it is off and vice versa. When Outline is on, the message "Outline" appears on the status line and certain keys operate as follows to create outlines:

- ENTER inserts a hard return and an outline number.

- TAB moves the outline number to the next tab stop and changes the outline number to the next level.

- MARGIN RELEASE (SHIFT+TAB) moves the outline number to the previous tab stop and changes the outline number to the previous level.

- ⇒INDENT (F4) or HOME, TAB locks the outline number in place and indents the text that follows to the next tab stop. (Press SPACEBAR if you wish to lock the outline number in place without indenting the text following the outline number to the next tab stop.)

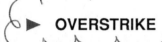

► OVERSTRIKE

FORMAT (SHIFT+F8) key
Other (4 or O)
Overstrike (5 or O)
Create (1 or C) or Edit (2 or E)

Prints two or more characters in the same position. Useful for inserting in a document special characters such as ≠ or è, which may not print on your printer with the Compose feature (see COMPOSE). The result is shown on the printed page; the Typing screen shows the last character only.

For the Create menu item, enter the characters that will print in the location where the cursor is located. For the Edit menu item, position the cursor forward from the overstrike you wish to alter before following the key sequence; the overstrike characters will appear for editing.

► PAGE BREAKS

Hard

CTRL+ENTER

Starts the cursor at the top of a new page, which is useful when you wish to end a short page of text, controlling where a page break will be. Also used to end a column and start a new one when working in text columns.

A page bar (a line of equal signs) across the Typing screen indicates the page break. The status line also reflects the change in page number.

Soft

No key sequence; performed by WordPerfect

Starts the cursor at the top of a new page after you type a complete page of text, determined by WordPerfect based on settings for top and bottom margins (see MARGINS), page length (see PAPER SIZE/TYPE), and line height (see LINE HEIGHT).

A page bar (a line of dashes) across the Typing screen indicates the page break. The status line reflects the change in page number. This page bar will readjust if text is later edited.

▶ PAGE FORMAT

See FORMAT

▶ PAGE NUMBERING

Insert Page Number in Text

FORMAT (SHIFT+F8) key
Page (2 or P)
Page Numbering (6 or N)
Insert Page Number (3 or I)

Inserts the page number at the cursor location in the current page number style (see *Style*).

Position

FORMAT (SHIFT+F8) key
Page (2 or P)
Page Numbering (6 or N)
Page Number Position (4 or P)

Turns on page numbering and selects the position where the page numbers will print, or turns off page numbering. Make sure that the cursor is at the top of the page before initiating this feature. The page numbers appear on the printed page and not on the Typing screen. Page numbers will appear in the current page number style (see *Style*).

There are nine options to choose from when selecting where to print page numbers: 1) top left, 2) top center, 3) top right, 4) top alternating left and right, 5) bottom left, 6) bottom center, 7) bottom right, 8) alternating left and right, or 9) no page numbering. (See SUPPRESS FOR CURRENT PAGE for the procedure to suppress page numbering for a specific page in a document. Also see HEADERS/FOOTERS for the procedure to insert page numbers as part of a header or footer.)

Style

FORMAT (SHIFT+F8) key
Page (2 or P)
Page Numbering (6 or N)
Page Number Style (2 or S)

Specifies the format for the page number when you turn on page numbering or insert the page number in a specific document. Press CTRL+B to insert ^B, which represents the page number itself. Text and codes can also be included in the page number style.

Renumber

See NEW PAGE NUMBER

► PAPER DEFINITIONS

Add

FORMAT (SHIFT+F8) key
Page (2 or P)
Paper Size/Type (7 or S)
Add (2 or A)

Creates a new paper definition for the currently selected printer. This definition contains information WordPerfect requires to print your text, such as the paper type, paper size, and location of the paper. During printing, WordPerfect uses this information whenever it encounters a paper size/type code in the document (see PAPER SIZE/TYPE), which specifies a particular paper definition.

WordPerfect displays a menu that lists the possible names for the type of paper you are defining. Select a paper type (such as envelopes, labels, transparencies, and so on) or select the menu item Other and enter a name of your own. Then define the paper's characteristics, including the following:

- Paper Size: The size (dimensions) of the paper.

- Paper Type: The type of paper (an opportunity to edit the name of the paper type).

- Font Type: The orientation of fonts used for printing, pertinent only for printers in which paper cannot be inserted sideways and instead where fonts can rotate—printing either in Portrait mode (where characters print parallel to the insertion edge of the paper) or Landscape mode (where characters print perpendicular to the insertion edge of the paper). For instance, the Landscape font type is used in laser printers for printing out an address on an envelope.

- Prompt to Load: Whether WordPerfect should pause before printing. If set to No, this implies that the paper is available in the printer. If set to Yes, WordPerfect will sound a beep so that you can insert paper; then select Go (4 or G) from the Control Printer screen to start the printing. (See also CONTROL PRINTER.)

- Location: The whereabouts of the paper during printing, either 1) a specified bin number (if the printer has a sheet feeder), 2) fed continuously (from one continuous form feeder, such as a paper tray, or using continuous-feed paper), or 3) fed manually.

- Double Sided Printing: Whether the text will print on both sides of the page (providing that your printer supports this feature).

- Labels: Whether the page will print text split by page breaks on screen onto the same piece of paper at the printer. If set to Yes, WordPerfect will be able to print addresses split by page breaks in your document onto one page (sheet) of labels. To do this, you must specify the following characteristics of the labels you will insert into the printer: the size of each individual label; the number of columns of labels across each page; the number of rows of labels down each page; the location at the top left corner of the first label where the printing should begin; the distance between each column of labels; the distance between each row of labels; and any margins you wish to specify for each individual label.

If you use single sheets of labels, make sure that the paper size is set to the actual dimensions of the sheet before defining the labels' characteristics. If you use continuous-feed rolls of labels, make sure that the paper size is set with the width equal to the distance between the left and right edges of the paper, and with the height equal to the distance between the top of one row of labels and the top of the next; then set the number of rows for continuous-feed labels to 1.

- Text Adjustment: The page offsets that are necessary to compensate for paper that is loaded into the printer at different horizontal or vertical positions than what WordPerfect assumes.

Manage

FORMAT (SHIFT+F8) key
Page (2 or P)
Paper Size/Type (7 or S)

Allows you to manipulate existing paper definitions. You can copy, delete, or edit a definition by positioning the cursor on the paper definition and selecting the appropriate menu item. For a deletion, type Y to verify.

PAPER SIZE/TYPE

FORMAT (SHIFT+F8) key
Page (2 or P)
Paper Size/Type (7 or S)
Position cursor on a paper definition
Select (1 or S)

Indicates to WordPerfect which pre-existing paper definition should be used to print out all or part of a document (see also PAPER DEFINITIONS). Text will adjust on screen if the selected paper definition results in a change in paper size. A change in paper type takes effect only at the printer. (When changing paper size, you may find that a modification in margins is also warranted.)

The cursor can be positioned on a paper definition that you wish to select either by using the arrow keys or by typing N to initiate the Name Search feature, typing the first letters of the paper type for that paper definition, and pressing ENTER. Select "[All Others]" and indicate a size for paper without a previously defined definition and for which you will create no new paper definition.

auto.

► PARAGRAPH NUMBERING

Define Numbering Style and Starting Number

See OUTLINING

Insert Paragraph Number

DATE/OUTLINE (SHIFT+F5) key
Para Num (5 or P)
ENTER or enter paragraph level

Inserts a paragraph number at the current cursor location.
When prompted with "Paragraph Level (Press Enter for Automatic)", press ENTER to set an automatic number, where the
paragraph level is determined by the location of the cursor in
relation to the tab stops. You also can type in a level number
and press ENTER to set a paragraph level regardless of the
cursor's current location.

► PASSWORD PROTECTION

See LOCK/UNLOCK FILES

► PATH FOR DOWNLOADABLE FONTS AND PRINTER FILES

See DOWNLOADABLE (SOFT) FONTS

► PITCH

See FONT and WORD/LETTER SPACING to alter the width of and amount of space between characters on the printed page. See DISPLAY PITCH to alter the pitch on screen.

► PREVIEW

See VIEW DOCUMENT

► PRINT

Block from Screen

Block the text
PRINT (SHIFT+F7) key
Y to confirm

Prints a highlighted block from the screen, which is useful if you wish to print only a portion of a page currently on screen, such as two paragraphs.

Document from Screen

PRINT (SHIFT+F7) key
Full Document (1 or F), Page (2 or P), or Multiple
    Pages (5 or M)

Prints one of the following for the document currently on screen: the full text which includes all pages; the page where the cursor is currently located; or multiple pages. For multiple pages, WordPerfect prompts "Page(s):", and you can enter a single page number (such as 5), a range of consecutive pages separated by a hyphen (such as 2-5), a range of nonconsecutive pages separated by a comma (such as 1,5,7), or the letter **s** to print out the document's summary if it has one. These options can be combined (such as s,3,9-14). Also, the absence of a number before a hyphen (such as -5) indicates printing should start at the first page, and the absence of a number after a hyphen (such as 8-) indicates printing should end at the last page.

Document on Disk

> PRINT (SHIFT+F7) key
> Document on Disk (3 or D)
> Enter filename
> Enter page numbers

or

> LIST (F5) key
> Type drive or directory name and press ENTER
> Position cursor on a file
> Print (4 or P)

Prints any number of pages of a document from disk. When WordPerfect prompts "Document Name:", make sure to precede the filename with the name of the drive or directory where the file is housed when it is not in the default.

When WordPerfect prompts "Page(s): (All)", press ENTER to print all pages of the document. To print out a specific page, type the page number and press ENTER. You can specify a range of consecutive pages using a hyphen (such as 4-8) or nonconsecutive pages using a comma (such as 1,4,9). Also, type **s** to print out the document's summary if it has one (see SUMMARY). These options can be combined (such as s, 3, 5-9). The absence of a number before a hyphen (such as -5) indicates that printing should start at the first page, and the absence of a number after a hyphen (such as 8-) indicates that printing should end at the last page.

▶ PRINT CHARACTERS

See FONT, APPEARANCE, and SIZE to learn how to alter the font or font attributes used to print out the characters of your document.

▶ PRINT COLORS

See COLORS, PRINT

▶ PRINT JOBS, CONTROL

See CONTROL PRINTER

► PRINT OPTIONS

SETUP (SHIFT+F1) key
Initial Settings (4 or I)
Print Options (8 or P)

Alters the default print options assumed for printing out documents for the currently selected printer, which Word-Perfect Corporation sets up to include the following:

Binding Width	0"
Number of Copies	1
Multiple Copies Generated by	WordPerfect
Graphics Quality	Medium
Text Quality	High
Redline Method	Printer Dependent
Size Attributes	Fine, 60%
(% of normal)	Small, 80%
	Large, 120%
	Very Large, 150%
	Extra Large, 200%
	Super/subscript, 60%

The size attributes represent the percent of what is the normal size for the base font. These attributes are dependent on the sizes available for the base font, and take effect only after you update your printer definition (see PRINTER DEFINI-TIONS).

When you change any of these print options in the Setup menu, the new settings remain as the default options for each subsequent use of WordPerfect.

See also BINDING, MULTIPLE COPIES, NUMBER OF COPIES, REDLINE, and TEXT/GRAPHICS QUALITY to learn how to alter those print options settings for print jobs in only the current working session.

▶ PRINT QUALITY

See TEXT/GRAPHICS QUALITY

▶ PRINT TO DISK

PRINT (SHIFT+F7) key
Select Printer (S)
Position cursor on printer name
Edit (3 or E)
Port (2 or P)
Other (8 or O)
Enter filename to be used for document printed to disk

Prints a document to a file on disk and is useful when you wish to print the document later with DOS commands on a printer located where WordPerfect is unavailable.

Once you follow the key sequence, return to your document. Make sure that you select the same printer name for printing your document as the one for which you altered the port. Print the document from the screen.

After printing to disk, be sure to follow the key sequence—this time selecting from one of the LPT or COM options on the Port menu (rather than the Other menu option). This resets WordPerfect to print to the printer, rather than to disk.

► PRINTER COMMANDS

FORMAT (SHIFT+F8) key
Other (4 or O)
Printer Functions (6 or P)
Printer Command (2 or P)
Command (1 or C) or Filename (2 or F)

Inserts a command into a document so that you can control special features of your printer. (Typically, printer commands are unnecessary because WordPerfect handles most of what you would use the commands to perform.) Printer commands are usually entered in decimal ASCII, as provided in the printer manual. Decimal codes less than 32 and greater than 126 must be entered in angle brackets, such as <15>.

Select the Command menu item if you will be inserting the commands from the keyboard. Select Filename and indicate the name of the file into which you previously saved those commands; that file will be downloaded when the document is sent to the printer. You indicate the pathname (drive or directory) for a file you plan to download to the printer in the same way you indicate the path for downloadable fonts (see *Path* in DOWNLOADABLE (SOFT) FONTS for the key sequence).

► PRINTER CONTROL

See CONTROL PRINTER

► PRINTER DEFINITIONS

Create

PRINT (SHIFT+F7) key
Select Printer (S)
Additional Printers (2 or A)
Position cursor on printer for which you wish to create a
definition
ENTER
Enter a filename for the printer file stored on disk or
press ENTER to accept WordPerfect's suggestion
Read over the Helps and Hints screen for that printer
EXIT (F7) key

Creates a printer definition (with the extension .PRS) that will
be used to select a printer and print out your documents. Select
Other Disk (2 or O) if, after selecting the Additional Printers
menu item, the name of your printer does not appear. When
WordPerfect prompts "Directory for printer files", type in the
drive or directory where other (previously installed) printer
files (with an extension .ALL) are housed. Then continue with
the key sequence shown. (To display more printers, you must
run the Installation program and install additional printer
files.)

After following the key sequence, you are ready to alter
any of the following printer settings that are incorrect:

* Name: Name that appears on the Print screen next to
  the item "Select Printer". A name can be up to 36
  characters in length.

- Port: Port (plug) where the printer is attached. LPT represents a parallel port, while COM represents a serial port.

- Sheet Feeder: Sheet feeder that is used to feed paper into your printer. If you use no sheet feeder, leave this option blank.

- Cartridges and Fonts: The fonts and cartridges you will use with your printer (see also CARTRIDGES AND FONTS).

- Initial Base Font: The default current font for your printer (see also FONT).

- Path for Downloadable Fonts and Printer Command Files: The drive or directory where files for downloadable fonts and printer commands are housed (see also DOWNLOADABLE (SOFT) FONTS and PRINTER COMMANDS).

Manage

PRINT (SHIFT+F7) key
Select Printer (S)
Position cursor on printer name
Edit (3 or E), Copy (4 or C), Delete (5 or D), Help (6 or H), or Update (7 or U)

Allows you to manipulate existing printer definitions. Edit, copy, or delete a printer definition, or use the Help option to display a Helps and Hints screen for that printer. Or use the Update option to upgrade a printer definition for changes.

▶ PRINTER FUNCTIONS

Instructs the printer how to handle unique printing situations
(see BASELINE PLACEMENT FOR TYPESETTERS,
KERNING, LEADING, PRINTER COMMANDS, WORD
AND LETTER SPACING, and WORD SPACING JUSTIFI-
CATION LIMITS).

▶ PRINTER, SELECT

PRINT (SHIFT+F7) key
Select Printer (S)
Position cursor on printer name
Select (1 or S)

Determines which printer among the printers that you previously defined will print the document on screen (see also
PRINTER DEFINITIONS). If you defined only one printer,
that printer is your only option.

Once a document is saved, the current printer selection is
saved with the document. The next time you retrieve or print
that document, from disk, WordPerfect formats that document for the saved printer selection (see also INITIAL SET-
TINGS).

▶ PROPORTIONAL SPACING

Proportional spacing alters the way in which characters are
spaced, so that characters occupy an amount of space proportional to their width. This can give a document a more

professional look. If your printer supports proportional spacing, then you activate it by the font that you select to print out your document. (See FONT for the key sequence.)

▶ PROTECT, BLOCK

> Block the text
> FORMAT (SHIFT+F8) key
> Y to confirm

Ensures that a block of text is not divided by a soft page break. This is useful to keep all lines of a table or chart on the same page. It is inserted automatically when typing in parallel columns with block protection to keep the parallel columns together and safe from a page break.

▶ PULL-DOWN MENUS

> ALT+=

Provides access to WordPerfect functions and features; an alternative to pressing function keys. If you have a mouse, you can instead display the menu bar by clicking the right mouse button.

A menu bar is displayed, from which you can "pull down" a menu. See the General Reference section for more information on the menus available. See DISPLAY for the procedure to alter the appearance of or access to these menus.

► QUALITY OF PRINT

See TEXT/GRAPHICS QUALITY

► RECOVER TEXT

See UNDELETE

► RECTANGLES

See APPEND, DELETE, and MOVE/COPY

► REFERENCES

See CROSS-REFERENCE

► REDLINE

Insert

Prints text with redline markings. Use this feature to mark characters of text that could possibly be added without fully committing yourself to adding the text.

See APPEARANCE for the key sequence to insert redline manually, or see DOCUMENT COMPARE for the key sequence to have WordPerfect compare two documents and insert redline automatically where text in the document on screen does not appear in the document on disk.

The redline markings are based on your printer and the redline method that you select (see *Method*).

Method

FORMAT (SHIFT+F8) key
Document (3 or D)
Redline Method (4 or R)
Printer Dependent (1 or P), Left (2 or L), or Alternating
   (3 or A)

Chooses how redline markings will appear on the printed page. The Printer Dependent menu item marks redlined text based on your printer's default option. Usually it is shading that appears over characters. Left marks redlined text with a horizontal bar or another character in the left margin. Alternating marks redlined text with a character in the left margin for even-numbered pages and in the right margin for odd-numbered pages. For those last two options, you enter the character of your choice when WordPerfect prompts "Redline Character:".

Remove Automatically

See REMOVE REDLINE AND STRIKEOUT

► REMOVE REDLINE AND STRIKEOUT

MARK TEXT (ALT+F5) key
Generate (6 or G)

Remove Redline Markings and Strikeout Text from
Document (1 or R)
Y to confirm

Removes all the redline markings and all the strikeout text
from the entire document on screen in one command. This is
useful to return to the edited version of a document after using
the Document Compare feature. Also useful after making
revisions using redline and strikeout and then deciding to
make those revisions permanent.

All redline codes are deleted. In addition, all strikeout
codes along with the text marked for strikeout are deleted.

► RENAME FILES

See MOVE/RENAME FILES

► REPEAT VALUE

ESCAPE (ESC) key
Type number of repetitions
Type character or command

Repeats a specified number of times either a character, a
macro, or the following cursor movement and deletion commands:

↑	PGUP
↓	PGDN
←	+ (numeric keypad)
→	− (numeric keypad)
CTRL+→	CTRL-BACKSPACE
CTRL+←	CTRL+END
DEL	CTRL+PGDN

When WordPerfect prompts "Repeat Value = 8", type in the number of repetitions. (The default setting is eight repetitions; if you want eight repetitions, there is no need to type in a number.) Type the character, execute a macro, or type a cursor movement command or a deletion command.

You can also change the default number of repetitions for a working session by pressing ESC, typing a number, and pressing ENTER; you can also change the default permanently (see INITIAL SETTINGS).

▶ REPLACE

REPLACE (ALT+F2) key
Y or N for Confirmation option
Type in search string
ESC or ⇒SEARCH (F2) or REPLACE (ALT+F2)
Type in replace string
ESC or ⇒SEARCH (F2) or REPLACE (ALT+F2)

Replaces a search string (word, code, or phrase) with a replace string (another word, code, or phrase), beginning at the cursor position and continuing to the end of the document. This is useful for altering repeated occurrences of text or codes or for deleting certain codes from the text. (Delete codes or text by leaving the replace string empty.)

If you select Confirmation, the program stops to ask for confirmation before replacing each occurrence in the text of the search string; otherwise, the replace occurs for the entire document in one operation.

If you insert letters as part of the search string, remember that uppercase letters in the search string match only uppercase in the text, while lowercase letters match either uppercase or lowercase. When the string in the text is capitalized, the replace string also will be capitalized. If you insert codes as part of the search or replace string, do so by following the same key sequence as when you insert that code into a document.

You can perform the replace on only a portion of a document by blocking text with the BLOCK (ALT+F4) key before beginning the key sequence.

You can extend the Replace feature to headers, footers, footnotes, endnotes, graphics box captions, and text boxes by pressing HOME before beginning the key sequence.

You can perform a replace in the reverse (backward) direction by pressing the up arrow key just before typing in the search string in the key sequence.

▶ RETRIEVE A FILE

By Typing a Filename

RETRIEVE (SHIFT+F10) key
Enter filename

Retrieves a copy of a file from disk onto the Typing screen for review, editing, or printing. Be sure to precede the filename by a path (drive or directory) if the file is stored in other than the default. If the file is locked, WordPerfect requests a password. WordPerfect 5.1, 5.0, and 4.2 files, as well as DOS text files, can be retrieved.

Should the Typing screen contain text, then the retrieved file is combined with the existing text on screen.

From a List of Files

> LIST (F5) key
> Type drive or directory name and press ENTER
> Position cursor on a file
> Retrieve (1 or R)

Retrieves a copy of a file from a certain directory or disk drive onto the Typing screen for review, editing, or printing. If the file is locked, WordPerfect requests a password. WordPerfect 5.1, 5.0, and 4.2 files, as well as DOS text files, can be retrieved.

Should the Typing screen contain text, then WordPerfect prompts for confirmation before combining the file on disk with the existing text on screen.

► RETURN

Hard

> ENTER

Moves the cursor down to the next line of text and is useful to end a short line of text, end a paragraph, or insert a blank line. (See also DISPLAY for the method to specify a character to represent a hard return on the Typing screen.)

If a soft return code is followed immediately by a hard return code, the hard return code is changed to a dormant hard return. This eliminates blank lines that appear at the top of a page or column.

Soft

No key sequence; performed by WordPerfect

Starts the cursor at the beginning of the next line after you type a full line of text. This is known as wordwrap. Where wordwrap occurs depends on the settings for features such as the left and right margins (see MARGINS) and the page width (see PAPER SIZE/TYPE). The line end will readjust if text is later edited.

REVEAL CODES

REVEAL CODES (ALT+F3) key

Splits the screen in half. The top window of the Reveal Codes screen shows the text as it appears on the Typing screen. The bottom window shows the same text along with the location of codes in that text. The two windows are separated by a ruler line. It is useful to reveal codes when you wish to determine whether a feature that only takes effect at the printer has been activated or to find the location of a code you wish to delete.

You can add or delete both text and codes while viewing the Reveal Codes screen.

The REVEAL CODES (ALT+F3) key operates like a toggle switch, so press it a second time to return to the Typing screen.

The size of the bottom window on the Reveal Codes screen can be changed; see DISPLAY.

▶ REWRITE SCREEN

See AUTOMATICALLY FORMAT AND REWRITE

▶ RULER LINE

SCREEN (CTRL+F3) key
Window (1 or W)
up arrow key and ENTER

Reduces the Typing screen's window by one, so that a ruler line can show current margin locations (brackets) and tab locations (triangles). This is useful when typing text on tab stops or when wishing to keep track of numerous tab stop and margin changes in one document.

To delete the ruler line, repeat the key sequence and press the down arrow key and ENTER as the last step in the key sequence.

▶ RUSH A PRINT JOB

See CONTROL PRINTER

▶ SAVE

Block

Block the text
SAVE (F10) key
Enter filename

Stores a copy of the highlighted text in a file of its own. This is useful if you wish to store just a part of a document on disk. If a file by that name already exists on disk, WordPerfect asks for confirmation to replace the old version with the new screen version.

Fast

See FAST SAVE

File (and Retain Document on Screen)

SAVE (F10) key
Enter filename

Stores a copy of the screen version of the document on disk. If a file by that name already exists on disk, WordPerfect asks for confirmation to replace the old version with the new screen version. Also, if you wish to save to a drive or directory other than the default, precede the filename with the other drive or directory name. After saving, the document remains on screen.

File (and Clear Screen)

EXIT (F7) key
Y to save document
Enter filename
Y or N to replace if filename already exists
N to clear screen and remain in WordPerfect

Stores a copy of the screen version of the document on disk. After saving, the screen clears, so you can begin a new document or retrieve an existing document. Also after saving, instead of typing N to clear the screen, you can press CANCEL (F1) to leave the document on screen or type Y to exit WordPerfect.

In DOS Text File Format

See DOS (ASCII) TEXT FILES

In Generic Word Processing Format

TEXT IN/OUT (CTRL+F5) key
Save As (3 or A)
Generic (1 or G)
Enter filename

Stores a file from the screen to disk in a generic word processing format, where the format of the document is maintained (although it is stripped of WordPerfect codes). This is useful for converting a document from WordPerfect into a document for another word processing package.

In WordPerfect 5.0 or 4.2 Format

TEXT IN/OUT (CTRL+F5) key
Save As (3 or A)
WP 5.0 (2 or W) or WP 4.2 (3 or P)
Enter filename

Stores a file from the screen to disk in version 5.0 or 4.2 format, so that it can be retrieved into an earlier WordPerfect version.

▶ SCREEN DISPLAY

See DISPLAY

▶ SCREEN SPLIT

See WINDOWS

▶ SEARCH

Forward   ⇒SEARCH (F2) key
            Type in search string
            ESC or ⇒SEARCH (F2)

Reverse   ⇐SEARCH (SHIFT+F2) key
            Type in search string
            ESC or ⇒SEARCH (F2)

Positions the cursor just past the next occurrence of the search string (word, code, or phrase) in the text. The forward search checks ahead in the text for the next occurrence, and the reverse search checks backward. This is useful for quickly moving the cursor to a certain title, phrase, or code in the document.

If you insert letters as part of the search string, remember that uppercase letters in the search string match only uppercase in the text, whereas lowercase letters match either uppercase or lowercase. If you insert codes as part of the search string, do so by following the same key sequence as when you insert that code into a document.

You can perform the search on only a portion of a document by blocking text before beginning the key sequence.

You can extend the Search feature to headers, footers, footnotes, endnotes, graphics box captions, and text boxes by pressing HOME before beginning the key sequence.

You can change your mind and perform a search in the reverse direction by pressing the up or down arrow key just before typing the search string in the key sequence.

▶ SEARCH AND REPLACE

See REPLACE

▶ SEARCH FOR A FILE

See FIND and NAME SEARCH

▶ SELECT

See SORT AND SELECT

▶ SELECT PRINTER

See PRINTER, SELECT

▶ SETUP

SETUP (SHIFT+F1) key

Alters a wide range of options for how WordPerfect operates when started up on your computer. A change in the Setup menu remains in effect each time you start WordPerfect and for all *new* documents. This is useful if you wish to tailor the operating of the WordPerfect program to your own special needs. (See also DISPLAY, ENVIRONMENT, INITIAL SETTINGS, KEYBOARD LAYOUT, LOCATION OF FILES, and MOUSE.)

▶ SHADOW

Prints text where characters appear twice; the second print is slightly offset from the first, based on the base font (see APPEARANCE for the key sequence).

▶ SHEET FEEDER

Defines the type of sheet feeder used with your printer (see PRINTER DEFINITIONS for the key sequence). You specify the sheet-feeder bin numbers where certain types of paper are located when you define the forms that will be used in your printer (see PAPER DEFINITIONS for the key sequence).

▶ SHELL

SHELL (CTRL+F1) key
Go to Shell (1 or G) or Retrieve Clipboard (2 or R)

If you have WordPerfect Library running, this allows you to go to the Shell menu or retrieve text from the clipboard. From Shell, you can exit temporarily to DOS. If Shell is not running, this key sequence exits you temporarily to DOS (see DOS, EXIT TO).

▶ SHORT/LONG DISPLAY

LIST (F5) key
ENTER
Short/Long Display (5 or S)
Short Display (1 or S) or Long Display (2 or L)
Type in drive or directory name and press ENTER

Allows you to switch between a list of files showing the files' short document names or a list showing the files' long document names. A short (DOS) document name consists of up to eight characters in the filename and up to three characters in the filename extension. (See the General Reminders section for a list of characters that can be used to name files with short names.) A long document name can contain up to 68 characters, including spaces and all characters (see LONG DOCUMENT NAMES for more details).

The short display lists twice as many files on screen as the long display. On the other hand, the long display lists more information—not only each file's short name, size, and revision date, but also its long document name and type. Once changed, the display selection is assumed for the rest of the working session or until you change it again.

SIZE

FONT (CTRL+F8) key
Size (1 or S)
Suprscpt (1 or P), Subscpt (2 or B), Fine (3 or F), Small
    (4 or S), Large (5 or L), Vry Large (6 or V), or Ext
    Large (7 or E)

For a particular base font, alters the attribute that controls the size of characters at the printer. Size attributes include Superscript, Subscript, Fine, Small, Large, Very Large, and Extra Large (see these separate entries for more details). Be aware that many printers do not support all of these size attributes for a given font.

To activate a size attribute as you type, follow the key sequence just shown and then select a menu item to turn on the desired size attribute. Next, type the text, and then turn off the size attribute either by 1) pressing the right arrow key, 2) repeating the same key sequence as when you turned on the attribute, or 3) pressing FONT and selecting Normal (3 or N) to turn off all attributes if more than one is active.

To activate a size attribute for existing text, use the Block feature to highlight the existing text before following the key sequence.

On screen, the text controlled by a given size attribute will be displayed in a different color or brightness to distinguish it from normal text (see COLORS/FONTS/ATTRIBUTES).

► SIZE ATTRIBUTE RATIOS

Determines the percent of the normal font size that text controlled by a given size attribute will take, and is most useful with PostScript printers. The size attributes include Fine, Small, Large, Very Large, Extra Large, Superscript, and Subscript. See PRINT OPTIONS for the appropriate key sequence.

► SMALL

Prints text in small size for the base font, which is <u>larger</u> than the Fine attribute but <u>smaller than normal</u> (see SIZE for the key sequence).

► SMALL CAPS

Prints text where all characters appear in capitals—either large for uppercase or small for lowercase—for the base font (see APPEARANCE for the key sequence).

171

► **SOFT FONTS**

See DOWNLOADABLE (SOFT) FONTS

► **SORT AND SELECT**

Block

Block the text
MERGE/SORT (CTRL+F9) key

Sorts and/or selects text contained in a highlighted block. The default is to sort the block line-by-line in ascending order (A to Z or smallest number to largest number) based on the first word in each line. If the text is within a table, the default is to sort the block row-by-row in ascending order based on the first word in the first line of the first cell. Change the sort defaults as described in *Entire Document*. Press Perform Action (1 or A) to begin the sort.

Entire Document

MERGE/SORT (CTRL+F9) key
Sort (2 or S)
ENTER or enter name of input file if document is not on screen
ENTER or enter name of output file if you want the results placed in a file on disk

Sorts an entire document, which can be on the screen or in a file on disk. You can sort lines, paragraphs, or secondary merge files into alphabetical or numeric order based on a specific word or field. You also can select records that meet a particular selection statement, where a record is each line (line sort), each paragraph (paragraph sort), or the data ending with an {END RECORD} code (merge sort). You can also perform both a sort and selection.

The default is to sort line-by-line in ascending order (A to Z or smallest number to largest number), based on the first word in each line, and not to select at all. Choose the Perform Action menu item (1 or P) to begin the sort assuming the default settings. Change the sort defaults before performing the action by choosing the following items from the Sort menu:

- Action: Specifies whether WordPerfect should perform a sort only, select only, or both. (You can only choose to select after having defined a selection statement.)

- Keys: Defines the characteristics of the word to be used in the sort or in a selection statement, including 1) alphanumeric or numeric; 2) the line number where the word is found (only for a paragraph or merge sort); 3) the field where the word is found, where a field is identified by the tab stop it is located on (line sort or paragraph sort), or as ending with an {END FIELD} code (merge sort); and 4) which word within the field. Define more than one key if you wish to sort on more than one word or if you wish to sort on certain words and select on other words. Specify the sort keys first (key1, key2, and so on) and the select keys last.

- Order: Specifies whether WordPerfect should sort in ascending order, which is A to Z or smallest to largest number, or descending order, which is Z to A and largest to smallest.

- Select: Defines a selection statement, the criteria on which text will be extracted, based on the defined keys. In the selection statement, refer to a key (such as key1 or key2) and use any of the following comparison symbols:

=	Equal to	< >	Not equal to
>	Greater than	>=	Greater than or equal to
<	Less than	<=	Less than or equal to

+	Or	(either part of the selection statement can be true for a record to be selected)
*	And	(both parts of the selection statement must be true for the record to be selected)

- Type: Specifies whether WordPerfect should sort lines, paragraphs, or records in a secondary merge file.

- View: Allows you to move the cursor up into the text about to be sorted.

When you change any of the sort or select defaults, they are altered until you change them again or until you exit WordPerfect.

Table

> Position cursor inside a table
> MERGE/SORT (CTRL+F9) key

Sorts and/or selects all rows in a table. The default is to sort the table row-by-row in ascending order (A to Z, or smallest number to largest number) based on the first word in the first line of the first cell. Change the sort defaults as described in *Entire Document*. Press Perform Action (1 or A) to begin the sort.

▶ SPACE, HARD

See HARD SPACE

▶ SPACING, LINE

See LINE SPACING

▶ SPACING, WORD AND LETTER

See WORD AND LETTER SPACING

▶ SPECIAL CHARACTERS

See COMPOSE

Check a Block

Block the Text
SPELL (CTRL+F2) key

Spell-checks a specific portion of a document on the screen against the dictionary on disk (see *Check a Word, Page, Entire Document* for options when a word is not found in the dictionary.)

Check a Word, Page, Entire Document

SPELL (CTRL+F2) key
Word (1 or W), Page (2 or P), or Document (3 or D)

Spell-checks a word, page, or whole document on screen against the dictionary on disk. After a page or document spell-check, WordPerfect performs a word count. When WordPerfect highlights a word not found in the dictionary, you have six options to choose from:

- Add: Adds the highlighted word to the supplementary dictionary, so that it will be treated as correctly spelled from that point on.

- Edit: Allows you to correct the highlighted word with the standard editing keys.

- Ignore Numbers: Tells WordPerfect to ignore all words containing a mix of letters and numbers for the rest of this spell-check.

- Look Up: Offers a list of additional words based on a word pattern that you type.

- Skip: Ignores the highlighted word for the rest of the spell-check.

- Skip Once: Ignores this one occurrence of the highlighted word.

The speller also pauses at words that appear in an irregular case (such as woRd), and you can choose to skip over the word, edit it, replace it, or disable irregular case-checking for the rest of the spell-check.

Count

See WORD COUNT

Drive/Directory Location

Specifies where the main dictionary and the supplementary dictionary are housed on disk (see LOCATION OF FILES).

Look Up

SPELL (CTRL+F2) key
Look Up (5 or L)
Enter word or word pattern

Looks up words in the dictionary that match a word or word pattern. Enter a word, and WordPerfect displays options that are phonetically similar. Enter a word pattern by using ? to represent a single letter and * to represent any number of letters in succession, and WordPerfect displays options that fit the pattern.

New Supplementary Dictionary

SPELL (CTRL+F2) key
New Sup. Dictionary (4 or N)

Specifies which supplementary dictionary to use in the current spell-check. This is useful if you maintain more than one supplementary dictionary. The primary supplemental dictionary, created when you first select the Add menu item from the Not Found menu and assumed unless you activate the New Supplementary Dictionary option, is a file that is named WP{WP}US.SUP (U.S. version).

► SPLIT SCREEN

See WINDOWS

► SPREADSHEET

Import

TEXT IN/OUT (CTRL+F5) key
Spreadsheet (5 or S)
Import (1 or I)

Retrieves a spreadsheet file that has been created in Plan-Perfect, Excel, or Lotus 1-2-3 (if saved in .WK1 format) into a WordPerfect document. This is a one-time retrieval, as opposed to the Link feature (See *Link*).

A Spreadsheet menu displays, where you can specify the following:

- Filename: The name of the spreadsheet file you wish to retrieve.

- Range: The range you wish to import, which is necessary if you wish to import only a section of the entire spreadsheet.

- Type: Whether to retrieve the spreadsheet as a table or as text formatted into tabular columns.

- Perform Import: Initiates the importing of the spreadsheet file according to the other specifications.

Link

TEXT IN/OUT (CTRL+F5) key
Spreadsheet (5 or S)
Create Link (2 or C) or Edit Link (3 or E)

Creates or edits a link between a spreadsheet file that has been created in PlanPerfect, Excel, or Lotus 1-2-3 (if saved in .WK1 format) and a WordPerfect document. The spreadsheet file is retrieved into the WordPerfect document on screen. The WordPerfect document can thereafter be updated whenever the spreadsheet file is altered. (See *Link Options*).

A Spreadsheet menu displays; specify how the link will be performed as described in *Import*.

Link Options

TEXT IN/OUT (CTRL+F5) key
Spreadsheet (5 or S)
Link Options (4 or L)

Allows you to specify whether links should be automatically updated when the WordPerfect document that contains links is retrieved; to initiate links manually if the updates are not automatic; and whether the display of link comments that surround the linked spreadsheets in the WordPerfect document should be hidden.

▶ START-UP (SLASH) OPTIONS

Loads WordPerfect and activates one or more special options at the same time, which can make your work with WordPerfect more efficient. Sometimes WordPerfect will not load properly without a start-up option. A start-up option takes effect until the next time you load WordPerfect. Rather than typing WP to load WordPerfect, type one of the following:

- **WP/CP=*codepage*** Indicates which code page your hardware system uses; important if your version of WordPerfect is not set to your code page. Code-page commands are 437, English; 850, PC Multilingual; 851, Greek; 8510, Greek Alternate; 860, Portuguese; 8600, Portuguese (Brazil); 861, Icelandic; 863, French (Canada); and 865, Norwegian and Dutch.

- **WP/D-*d:*** Redirects WordPerfect's temporary files to another drive, where d: is the drive (such as B:).

- **WP *filename*** Retrieves the file specified as soon as WordPerfect is loaded.

- **WP/M-*macroname*** Executes the macro specified as soon as WordPerfect is loaded.

- **WP/NB** Specifies that no .BK! backup file is created, even temporarily, when you choose to replace a file on disk with the document on screen.

- **WP/NC** Disables the Cursor Speed feature, which may conflict with certain equipment or with other software loaded before WordPerfect (see also CURSOR SPEED).

- **WP/NE** Inhibits the use of expanded memory when using WordPerfect.

- **WP/NF** Activates a nonflash option in the event that your screen periodically goes blank or you use a windowing program.

- **WP/NK** Disables enhanced keyboard commands that may conflict with certain equipment or other software loaded before WordPerfect.

- **WP/NO** Disallows the key combination CTRL+6 from being used to return the keyboard to its original mapping.

- **WP/PS=*path*** Tells WordPerfect the location of, and your desire to use, a .SET (setup) file that is in a directory other than where the WordPerfect WP.EXE program file is housed.

- **WP/W=*cm,em*** Specifies the amount of conventional and expanded memory to be used by WordPerfect (*cm* = conventional memory, *em* =

expanded memory). Type **WP/W=*.*** to use all available conventional and expanded memory.

- **WP/R** Speeds up operations of the WordPerfect program; available only if your computer is equipped with expanded memory and at least 300K RAM is unused.

- **WP/SS=*r,c*** Sets the rows and columns of your monitor if WordPerfect is unable to detect the proper size (*r* = rows that your screen supports, *c* = columns that your screen supports). Add the /F2 option if you still have problems.

- **WP/X** Loads WordPerfect and restores the original default settings as defined by WordPerfect Corporation, despite any changes to defaults made with the Setup menu (as described in SETUP).

▶ STATUS LINE DISPLAY

See UNITS OF MEASURE

▶ STOP PRINTING

See PRINTER CONTROL

▶ STRIKEOUT

Insert

Prints the text with strikeout markings, usually a line through the text marked for strikeout. Use this text attribute when you wish to mark characters of text that could possibly be deleted, without actually deleting the text.

See APPEARANCE for the key sequence to insert strikeout manually, or see DOCUMENT COMPARE for the key sequence to have WordPerfect compare two documents and insert strikeout marks automatically wherever text in the document on disk does not appear in the document on screen.

Remove

See REMOVE REDLINE AND STRIKEOUT

▶ STYLES

Create/Edit a Style

STYLE (ALT+F8) key
Position cursor on style name (only if editing)
Create (3 or C) or Edit (4 or E)

Defines the combination of formatting codes and/or text that make up a style, which can then be used to format certain elements in a document. Or, edits a previously created style definition. The following are options on the Styles Edit screen that appears when you create or edit a style:

- Name: The style name, which will be used when you wish to turn on or off a style in the text.

- Type: Specifies whether the style will be paired, (where the style has a beginning and end so that it effects a particular block of text) or open (which has only a beginning and is not turned off).

  A third alternative is to indicate an outline style, which is actually a collection of as many as eight "substyles"—one style for each outline level (see OUTLINING for a discussion on using the Outline feature). Each of the eight substyles within an outline style can be either open or paired. When you choose the Outline type from the Styles Edit screen, WordPerfect requests a level number. Type in a level number, and an Outline Styles Edit screen appears; the characteristics already assigned on the Styles Edit screen are now assigned to the substyle of the level number that you indicated. On the Outline Styles screen, you can now define the Name, Type, Description, Codes, and Enter options for all eight of the substyles, each of which corresponds to another outline level.

- Description: Describes the formatting task accomplished by the style, which can be up to 54 characters in length.

- Codes: Allows you to insert the codes and text that compose the style. WordPerfect displays a Reveal Codes screen. For an open style, the screen is blank, and codes and text should be inserted as in a document. For a paired style, the screen contains a comment code. Place any codes/text that will be inserted when the style is turned on before the comment code, and place any codes/text that will be inserted when the style is turned off after the comment code.

• Enter: Determines whether, after turning on a style, pressing the ENTER key will insert a hard return, turn off the style, or turn it off and then on again. Pertinent only if you are defining a paired type of style.

If you turn on a style in the text (see *Turn On/Off*) and then edit the style definition, the text affected by that style will automatically update to reflect the new style definition.

An outline style can also be created or edited from the same screen that allows you to turn on an outline style (see *Turn On/Off*).

Delete a Style

STYLE (ALT+F8) key
Position cursor on style name
Delete (5 or D)

Deletes a previously created style. You must indicate whether you wish to: leave the codes, which means the style and the style codes are erased but the text/codes that comprise that style remain in the text; include the codes, which means the style, style codes, and text/codes that comprise the style are erased; or erase the definition only, which means that if any style codes corresponding to that style definition are in the text, the definition will be recreated.

Establish a Style Library

Signifies that a certain list of styles saved into its own file (see *Save/Retrieve a Style*) acts as your style library (see LOCATION OF FILES for the key sequence).

Once you establish a style library, that list of styles is then automatically attached to every new document that you subsequently create. To attach the style library to a previously existing document, retrieve the file to screen, press STYLES (ALT-F8), and select the Update item from the Styles menu.

Save/Retrieve a Style

STYLE (ALT+F8) key
Save (6 or S) or Retrieve (7 or R)

Typically, styles are saved along with the document in which they were created. You can, however, save a list of styles into a separate file and then retrieve that list into any other document. Use this when you create styles for one document and wish to use these same styles in other documents.

When WordPerfect prompts "Filename:", enter a name for the list of files you wish to save or retrieve.

Turn On/Off

Not outline   STYLE (ALT+F8) key
style   Position cursor on style name
                  On (1 or O) or Off (2 or F)

Outline style	DATE/OUTLINE (SHIFT+F5) key
	Define (6 or D)
	Outline Style Name (9 or N)
	Position cursor on outline style name
	Select (1 or S)

An open style is turned on but not off; the style affects the text from the current cursor position to the end of the document (or until other codes of the same type as is found in the style definition are inserted further forward in the text). An outline style is turned on (selected) but is also not turned off; the outline style changes if, further forward in the document, you either turn on a different outline style or define a new numbering style (see OUTLINING).

A paired style is turned both on and off. If you have yet to type the text to be governed by the style, then turn on the style, type the text, and then turn off the style. (If a paired style is defined where the ENTER key turns off a style, then, to turn off the style, simply press ENTER rather than following the key sequence.) If you have already typed the text to be governed by the style, use the BLOCK (ALT+F4) key to block the text before following the key sequence. The style will be turned on in front of the blocked text and turned off after the text.

When the cursor is positioned on a style code, the code expands on the Reveal Codes screen to display the text/codes that define the style.

▶ SUBDOCUMENTS

See MASTER DOCUMENTS

► SUMMARY, DOCUMENT

Create/Edit

FORMAT (SHIFT+F8) key
Document (3 or D)
Summary (5 or S)

Offers an efficient method for keeping track of the contents
and history of a document. The summary is a fill-in-the-
blanks form, where the following information is either inserted by WordPerfect or can be entered by you: creation date,
which is the date that the summary was created and is inserted
by WordPerfect; document name/type, which can be entered
by you as a descriptive name or can be inserted by Word-
Perfect if the Long Document Name feature is activated and
the document has been assigned a long document name (See
LONG DOCUMENT NAME); author/typist, which Word-
Perfect can insert if you previously entered this information
for another document; subject, which WordPerfect can insert
(see *Subject Search Text*); account; keywords; and abstract,
which WordPerfect can insert as the first 400 characters from
the document. To capture the author/typist, subject, and abstract information, press RETRIEVE (SHIFT+F10) when viewing
the document summary.

An existing document summary can be viewed or edited
by repeating the key sequence. A document summary is also
displayed when you use the Look feature to view the contents
of a file on disk (see LOOK).

When viewing a document summary, press DEL to erase
the summary or press SAVE (F10) to save it into a file.

Display Automatically

SETUP (SHIFT+F1) key
Environment (3 or E)
Document Management Summary (4 or D)
Create on Save/Exit (1 or C)
Y or N

Tells WordPerfect whether or not to prompt you for a document summary when you use the SAVE or EXIT key to save a brand-new document. Type **Y** to turn on the feature or **N** to turn it off. When on, this feature reminds you to create a document summary for each new document.

Subject Search Text

SETUP (SHIFT+F1) key
Environment (3 or E)
Document Management/Summary (4 or D)
Subject Search Text (2 or S)

Identifies for WordPerfect the subject search string, which is used by WordPerfect to fill out the subject entry of a new document summary when you press RETRIEVE to capture that information. The default is "RE:".

▶ SUPER/SUBSCRIPT

Directs the printer to position characters slightly above (superscript) or below (subscript) the standard line of text and is useful in equations and other statistical typing. WordPerfect uses this feature automatically to print out footnote and endnote reference numbers in the text. (See SIZE for the key sequence.) On some printers, superscript and subscript text will also print smaller than the normal size.

► SUPPRESS FOR CURRENT PAGE

FORMAT (SHIFT+F8) key
Page (2 or P)
Suppress (8 or U)

Suppresses page numbering, headers, and/or footers for the current page by choosing one of eight different options. Use it for suppressing these features on the first page of a letter or report, or on a single page containing a table or chart.

► SWITCH BETWEEN UPPERCASE AND LOWERCASE

See CASE CONVERSION

► SWITCH WINDOWS

See WINDOWS

► SUPPLEMENTARY DICTIONARY

See SPELL

▶ TAB ALIGN

Use

TAB ALIGN (CTRL+F6) key

Vertically aligns text or numbers on a decimal/align character at the next tab stop. For example, if the decimal/align character is the decimal point (period), you can align a column of numbers on the decimal point. (See also DECIMAL/ALIGN CHARACTER to learn how to change the decimal/align character.)

When WordPerfect prompts "Align char =", type the tab entry. When the decimal/align character is typed, the prompt disappears. (If this character is not typed, then the entry is aligned flush right on the tab stop.)

Set Alignment Character

See DECIMAL/ALIGN CHARACTER

▶ TABLES

Create

COLUMNS/TABLES (ALT+F7) key
Tables (2 or T)
Create (1 or C)
Enter number of columns
Enter number of rows

Defines the basic table structure. WordPerfect automatically creates evenly spaced columns in a grid pattern based on the current margin settings. Each intersection of a column and row in the grid is referred to as a cell. Cells are labeled alphabetically from left to right in each row (A,B,C, and so on) and numerically from top to bottom(1,2,3, and so on) in each column, so that the first cell in the upper-left corner is labeled A1. Default settings are for double lines to border the outside of the table, single lines to border the inside, and for text within each cell to be left-justified. (See *Edit* to alter these and other table options.) Press EXIT (F7) when you are done editing the table structure and are ready to type text into the table.

Delete/Insert

Position cursor within table
COLUMNS/TABLES (ALT+F7) key
Position cursor on cell in row or column
DEL or INS
Rows (1 or R) or Columns (2 or C)
Enter number of rows or columns

Deletes or inserts the number of rows or columns that you specify. If you delete, both the contents of the cells as well as the cells themselves are deleted. You can instead delete the contents of a block of cells without deleting the actual cells. Follow steps 1 and 2 in the key sequence to return to the Table Edit menu, and then proceed as follows: block the cells, press MOVE (CTRL+F4), and select from the menu displayed to delete a block.

Edit/Perform Math

Position cursor within table
COLUMNS/TABLES (ALT+F7) key

or

Position cursor below table
COLUMNS/TABLES (ALT+F7) key
Tables (2 or T)
Edit (2 or E)

Displays the Table Edit menu, allowing you to change default settings for the table structure and to perform mathematical calculations in the table. Before selecting from the Table Edit menu, position the cursor appropriately. To alter settings or activate math for a single cell, position the cursor on that cell; for a column or row, position the cursor on any cell in that column or row; for a group of cells, use the Block feature to highlight that group. Options on the Table Edit menu include

- Size: Redefines the number of rows or columns that comprise the table.

- Format: Sets the design characteristics for either a column or for cells, including the vertical alignment, justification, and font attributes; or sets the maximum number of lines and line height for rows.

- Lines: Determines the style of lines that border a cell or block of cells.

- Header: For a table that spans many pages, establishes one or more header rows that are repeated automatically at the top of each page.

- Math: Performs mathematic calculations in a table. Select Calculate to determine the result of all formulas entered into the table. Select Formula to enter a formula into a specific cell; a formula can contain numbers, references to other cells (such as A1 or B2), and/or the following symbols:

+	Addition
−	Subtraction
*	Multiplication
/	Division

  Select Copy Formula to copy a formula from one cell to others, where all cell references in that formula are copied relatively. Or select from three math operators for calculating down a column:

+	Subtotal
=	Total
*	Grand Total

- Options: Defines the spacing between text and the lines that border the cells, how negative numbers are displayed when calculated, the location of the table on the page, and the shading of cells.

- Join: Combines multiple cells from adjoining rows into one cell.

- Split: Splits a cell into multiple cells.

Move Between Cells

See the General Reminders section

Move/Copy Cells

Position cursor within table
COLUMNS/TABLES (ALT+F7) key
Block the cells or position cursor in the row or column
MOVE (CTRL+F4) key
Block (1 or B), Row (2 or R) or Column (3 or C)
Move (1 or M) or Copy (2 or C)
Reposition cursor
ENTER

Moves or copies one cell, a block of cells, a row, or a column. For a block, text is moved or copied into pre-existing cells and overwrites the contents of those cells. For a row or column, a new row or column is created when it is moved or copied.

Type Text In

Type text into cells in any order

When the cursor is located in a table, the status line contains a cell indicator, such as

Cell A1 Doc 1 Pg 1 Ln 1.14" Pos 1.12"

After typing text into a cell, use the arrow keys to move the cursor to the next cell in the arrow's direction, or press TAB to move to the next cell and SHIFT+TAB to move to the previous cell.

► TABLES OF AUTHORITIES

Define

MARK TEXT (ALT+F5) key
Define (5 or D)
Define Table of Authorities (4 or A)
Enter section number

Defines the location and style options for one section of a table of authorities (citations) when it is generated. You can define up to 16 sections for a table of authorities. Once you specify a section number, a Table of Authorities Definition screen for that section appears, offering the following style options: whether page numbers, which will appear flush right, should be preceded by dot leaders; whether to allow underlining; and whether blank lines should be inserted between authorities. These style options can also be altered more permanently (see *Initial Settings*).

Edit Full Form

MARK TEXT (ALT+F5) key
Define (5 or D)
Edit Table of Authorities Full Form (5 or E)

Edits an authority after the full form has already been marked (see *Mark Text For*).

Generate

Generates a table of authorities after you have marked the text for the table and defined the table. Up to 16 sections of the table of authorities can be generated, one for each table of authorities definition mark inserted in the document. (See GENERATE CROSS-REFERENCES, ENDNOTES, INDEXES, LISTS, TABLES for the key sequence.)

Initial Settings

> SETUP (SHIFT+F1) key
> Initial Settings (4 or I)
> Table of Authorities (7 or A)

Determines the default options that will be used when the table of authorities is generated. Change any of the three style options as explained in *Define*.

Mark Text For

Full form	Block the text
	MARK TEXT (ALT+F5) key
	ToA (4 or A)
	Enter section number
	Type and edit the authority
	EXIT (F7) key
	Enter short form
Short form	MARK TEXT (ALT+F5) key
	ToA Short Form (4 or A)
	Enter short form

Marks the citation you wish to be included in a table of authorities when generated. The full form method is used the first time you mark a citation in a document; how you type and edit the full form is how that citation will appear in the table of authorities. The short form method is used for the second and all future occurrences of that citation. The full

form and short form for the same citation are linked together
with the same short form text.

▶ TABLES OF CONTENTS

Define

> MARK TEXT (ALT+F5) key
> Define (5 or D)
> Define Table of Contents (1 or C)

Defines the location and style options of the table of contents
when it is generated. When you follow the key sequence, a
Table of Contents Definition screen appears, offering style
options for how many levels the table will contain, whether
or not the last level will be wrapped, and which numbering
style will be used when the table is generated.

Generate

Generates a table of contents after you have marked the text
for the table and defined the table (see GENERATE CROSS-
REFERENCES, ENDNOTES, INDEXES, LISTS, TABLES
for the key sequence).

Mark Text For

> Block the text
> MARK TEXT (ALT+F5) key
> ToC (1 or C)
> Enter table of contents level number

Marks the word or phrase you wish to be included in a table of contents when generated.

▶ TABS

Set

FORMAT (SHIFT+F8) key
Line (1 or L)
Tab Set (8 or T)

Changes the location of tab stops and is used to change where the first line of a paragraph is indented, or to design a chart of aligned text/numbers.

A ruler line shows the current tab stop locations. To erase the current tab stops from the cursor to the end of the tab ruler line, press DELETE EOL (CTRL+END). To delete one tab stop, position the cursor and press DEL.

When setting tabs, you can choose from one of seven different tab stop styles: left-justified (the default tab style), left-justified with a dot leader, right-justified, right-justified with a dot leader, decimal, decimal with a dot leader, or center. To set one tab stop, position the cursor on the ruler line and type **L** (or press TAB), **R**, **C**, or **D** to specify a tab stop style. Then type a period if you desire a dot leader for that style. To set evenly spaced tab stops, type the starting position and the increment measurement, separated by a comma (such as 1",0.5"). For evenly spaced tab stops, WordPerfect assumes the left-justified style unless the starting position contains a tab of another style.

Tabs can be set in either of two ways: relative type or absolute type. Relative means that the tabs are set relative to the left *margin,* so that tab locations adjust to remain the same distance from the left margin if the left margin setting is changed. Absolute means that tabs are set absolute with respect to the left *edge* of the paper form, and not the left margin, so that the tab locations stay fixed if the left margin setting is changed. When you select relative type, the ruler line displays + and − signs next to the measurements that are to the left and right of the left margin. With absolute type, the + and − signs disappear.

Use

TAB key

Positions the cursor at the next tab stop. If the next tab is left-justified, all text typed on that tab stop to the end of that line is aligned against the tab stop. For a right-justified tab stop, all text is aligned flush right against the tab stop. For a center tab stop, the text is centered over the tab stop. For a decimal tab stop, the decimal (or other decimal/align character) typed as part of the entry is aligned on the tab stop. If that tab style has a dot leader, a row of dots will display from the point where you pressed the TAB key up to the tab stop.

If you press HOME before pressing TAB, you can left-align text at the next tab stop regardless of the style of tab setting. Moreover, other keys in addition to TAB operate on tab stops to align text in different ways. If you press HOME before pressing either CENTER, FLUSH RIGHT, or TAB ALIGN, you can insert a center, right, or decimal-aligned tab at the current tab setting regardless of the style of that tab setting (see also

CENTER, INDENT, MARGIN RELEASE, and TAB ALIGN).

▶ TABULAR COLUMNS

See TABS to set or use tab stops for creating tabular columns. See also MOVE/COPY, DELETE, and APPEND.

▶ TARGETS

See CROSS-REFERENCE

▶ TEXT COLUMNS

Define

COLUMNS/TABLES (ALT+F7) key
Columns (1 or C)
Define (3 or D)
Type (1 or T)
Newspaper (1 or N), Parallel (2 or P), or Parallel with
    Block Protect (3 or B)
Number of Columns (2 or N)
Enter number of columns
Distance Between Columns (3 or D) or Margins (4
or M)

Defines your column layout, the first basic step to creating columns. You define from 2 to 24 columns, choosing one of three types: newspaper, where text flows down a column all the way to the bottom of the page and then starts at the top of the next; parallel, where related text remains together in short, adjacent columns across the page; and parallel with Block Protect, which are similar to parallel columns except that no column entry will be split by a page break.

For the Distance Between Columns menu item, you enter a distance between columns; WordPerfect will calculate the left and right margins for evenly spaced columns automatically. For Margins, you can manually enter the location for each column's left and right margin.

See also TABLES as an alternative to parallel columns.

Display

SETUP (SHIFT+F1) key
Display (2 or D)
Edit Screen Options (6 or E)
Side-by-Side Columns Display (7 or S)
Y or N

Determines whether columns are displayed side-by-side on the screen or each on a separate page. Setting side-by-side display off is useful when editing text within columns because it speeds up WordPerfect's response time.

Type **Y** to turn on side-by-side display, or type **N** to turn it off. Your selection has no effect on the printed text: columns are always printed side-by-side.

Move Cursor Between

See the General Reminders section.

Type Text In (Newspaper)

Type complete text

Formats text into the newspaper-style column layout that you defined. Be sure to define your columns and turn columns on before typing the text.

When a page's bottom margin is reached, the cursor moves to the top of the next column so you can continue typing. When a page's bottom margin is reached in the last column, the cursor moves to the top of the first column on the next page.

To end a column before the bottom margin is reached, press HARD PAGE (CTRL+END); the cursor moves to the top of the next column or to the top of the first column on a new page.

Type Text In (Parallel)

Type text of one short, adjacent column
HARD PAGE (CTRL+ENTER) key

Formats text into the parallel-style column layout that you defined. Be sure to define your columns and turn columns on before typing the text.

Each group of adjacent columns across the page is typed before continuing with the next group of adjacent columns. WordPerfect automatically inserts a blank line between each group of parallel (adjacent) columns.

Turn On/Off

COLUMNS/TABLES (ALT+F7) key
Columns (1 or C)
On (1 or O) or Off (2 or F)

Turns Column mode on if it was off or vice versa. Turn Column mode on after defining your columns, but before typing the text that will be formatted into columns. (In order to turn on columns, your cursor must be forward from a [Col Def:] code.) Turn Column mode off after typing the text.

When the cursor is located in a portion of the document where Column mode is on, the status line contains a column indicator, such as

Col 1 Doc 1 Pg 1 Ln 1" Pos 1"

▶ TEXT/GRAPHICS QUALITY

PRINT (SHIFT+F7) key
Graphics Quality (G) or Text Quality (T)
Do Not Print (1 or N), Draft (2 or D), Medium (3 or M),
    or High (4 or H)

Print options that determine the quality level with which text and/or graphics will be printed. This is useful to print out draft copies quickly or to print out text and graphics in separate printings (for printers that cannot print text and graphics in the same print job).

The higher the quality, the better the resolution on the printed page and thus the longer it takes for the printer to complete the print job. (Be aware that for some printers, the menu items Draft, Medium, and High have no effect on the output.)

► TEXT SCREEN TYPE

See DISPLAY

► THESAURUS

Position cursor on word
THESAURUS (ALT+F1) key

Provides synonyms and antonyms for the highlighted word. Use the arrow keys to move the cursor within the list of synonyms and antonyms and between the three columns of words displayed. The following options are available on the Thesaurus menu:

- Clear Column: Clears the list of synonyms and antonyms for the last word selected.

- Look Up Word: Allows you to look up synonyms and antonyms for another word.

- Replace Word: Substitutes the word corresponding to the letter you select for the highlighted word.

- View Doc: Allows you to move the cursor up into the text to peruse the document before making a word selection.

► THOUSANDS' SEPARATOR

FORMAT (SHIFT+F8) key
Other (4 or O)
Decimal/Align Character (3 or D)

Alters the character used to separate the thousands' digits
when using the Math feature (see also MATH COLUMNS).
The default is the comma. Before entering a thousands'
separator, you enter a decimal/align character (see also DEC-
IMAL/ALIGN CHARACTER).

► TRANSFER FILES TO/FROM WORDPERFECT

See CONVERT FILES TO/FROM WORDPERFECT,
SAVE, and SPREADSHEET

► TYPEOVER MODE

INS key

In Typeover mode, characters you type will replace (type
over) existing characters. INS is a toggle switch, which shifts
the way WordPerfect edits text between Insert and Typeover
modes. The initial setting is Insert mode (see also INSERT
MODE). When in Typeover mode, the message "Typeover"
appears on the status line.

► UNDELETE (UNDO)

CANCEL (F1) key
Restore (1 or R) or Previous Deletion (2 or P)

If no menu or prompt is on the screen, recovers any of the last three deletion levels, where a deletion level is a group of consecutive deletions. A deletion level is shown highlighted at the current cursor position. The Restore menu item reinserts the highlighted text at the current cursor position, while the Previous Deletion menu item shows another of the last three deletion levels as highlighted text.

If you have a mouse, you can also access this feature by clicking the middle mouse button or by clicking the left and right mouse buttons simultaneously.

► UNDERLINE

Using the Underline Key

UNDERLINE (F8) key

Produces characters that are underlined with a single underscore when printed. On screen, the underlined text may display underscored or in a different color or brightness to distinguish it from normal text. (See also the section COLORS/FONTS/ATTRIBUTES to set the way the underline attribute is displayed on screen.)

To activate underlining as you type, press UNDERLINE (F8), type the text, and then press UNDERLINE (F8) a second time or press the right arrow key to turn off underline. (The UNDER-

LINE key is a toggle switch; it turns underline on if it was off or vice versa.)

To activate underlining for existing text, use the Block feature to highlight the existing text before pressing UNDER-LINE (F8).

To underline with a double underscore, see DOUBLE UNDERLINE. To alter the way in which the Underline feature operates, see UNDERLINE SPACES AND TABS.

Using the Font Key

Allows a second method for underlining characters (see AP-PEARANCE).

► UNDERLINE SPACES AND TABS

FORMAT (SHIFT+F8) key
Other (4 or O)
Underline Spaces/Tabs (7 or U)
Y or N to underline spaces
Y or N to underline tabs

Determines how underlining will appear on the printed page. You can request that WordPerfect underline spaces, tabs, both spaces and tabs, or neither spaces nor tabs that are between a beginning and ending underline code.

▶ UNITS OF MEASURE

SETUP (SHIFT+F1) key
Environment (3 or E)
Units of Measure (8 or U)

Alters the way measurements are displayed in two circumstances: on the status line, and for features that require a measurement entry (such as margins, tabs, line height, and so on). Your options include inches (either " or i), centimeters (c), points (p), 1200ths of an inch (w), or WordPerfect 4.2 vertical and horizontal units (u).

Regardless of the measurement you select as the default, you can enter measurements in a different unit. After typing the number measurement, type in a letter that indicates the unit you are using. For example, you can indicate a specific margin as 1.5" (inches), 2.5c (centimeters), 90p (points), 1500w (1200ths of an inch), 15h (version 4.2 horizontal units, appropriate when setting a left or right margin), or 15v (version 4.2 vertical units, appropriate when setting a top or bottom margin). WordPerfect will convert your entry into the default unit of measurement.

▶ VERY LARGE

Prints text in very large size for the base font, where very large is smaller than extra large but bigger than large (see SIZE for the key sequence).

▶ VIEW DOCUMENT

PRINT (SHIFT+F7) key
View Document (6 or V)

Displays the format of the document on the screen, indicating
as accurately as possible how it will appear when printed.
Features such as justification, headers, footers, page numbering, line numbering, and margins are shown. Depending on
your monitor and graphics card, fonts and font attributes can
also be displayed. Use this feature to preview a document
before printing.

Once you are viewing the document, use the cursor movement keys to view different pages of the text. Also, you can
alter how the View screen displays with options for 100%
(actual size), 200% (twice actual size), full page, or facing
pages (to see two full pages of text at once).

▶ WIDOW/ORPHAN PROTECTION

FORMAT (SHIFT+F8) key
Line (1 or L)
Widow/Orphan Protection (9 or W)
Y or N

Ensures that one line of a paragraph is not stranded on a
separate page due to a soft page break. With Widow/Orphan
Protection set to Yes (turned on), a page break may occur one
line earlier or one line later to keep the first or last line together
with the rest of the paragraph.

► WINDOWS

Split

SCREEN (CTRL+F3) key
Window (1 or W)
Type number of lines or use the up or down arrow keys
ENTER

Splits the screen into two windows separated by a ruler line. The top window contains Doc 1, and the bottom window contains Doc 2. This feature is useful when you wish to refer to or copy from one document while typing another, or for comparing the contents of two documents.

To again view only one window, repeat the key sequence but enter the number of lines as 0 or as the full size of the screen (24 for a standard-sized monitor) when WordPerfect prompts for the number of lines in the window.

Switch

SWITCH (SHIFT+F3) key

Moves the cursor between the Doc 1 and Doc 2 window. The status line indicates which document is on the screen. You can work with two documents on two separate screens, switching back and forth, or work with two documents on one split screen (see *Split*).

▶ WORD AND LETTER SPACING

FORMAT (SHIFT+F8) key
Other (4 or O)
Printer Functions (6 or F)
Word/Letter Spacing (3 or W)

Adjusts the spacing between adjacent words and letters. Options include Normal (spacing that looks best according to the printer manufacturer), Optimal (spacing that looks best according to WordPerfect Corporation), Percent of Optimal (enter a percentage—numbers less than 100% reduce the spacing), and Set Pitch (enter a pitch in characters per inch).

▶ WORD COUNT

SPELL (CTRL+F2) key
Count (6 or C)

Counts the number of words in the document. It can also be used to count the words in a highlighted block of text if you use the Block feature to highlight the text to be counted before following the key sequence.

► WORD SPACING JUSTIFICATION LIMITS

FORMAT (SHIFT+F8) key
Other (4 or O)
Printer Functions (6 or P)
Word Spacing Justification Limits (4 or J)

When justification is full, determines how much WordPerfect expands or compresses spacing between words to justify a line. Once a spacing is reached between words, WordPerfect adjusts the spacing between characters.

Enter a compression and an expansion percentage (anything over 999% implies unlimited expansion).

INDEX